CULTURAL

STUDIES

Volume 1　Number 1　January 1987

CULTURAL STUDIES is a new international journal, dedicated to the notion that the study of cultural processes, and especially of popular culture, is important, complex, and both theoretically and politically rewarding. It is published three times a year, with issues being edited in rotation from Australia, the UK and the USA, though occasional issues will be edited from elsewhere (e.g. one from Italy in 1988). Its international editorial collective consists of scholars representing the range of the most influential disciplinary and theoretical approaches to cultural studies.

CULTURAL STUDIES will be in the vanguard of developments in the area worldwide, putting academics, researchers, students and practitioners in different countries and from diverse intellectual traditions in touch with each other and each other's work. Its lively international dialogue will take the form not only of scholarly research and discourse, but also of new forms of writing, photo essays, cultural reviews and political interventions.

CULTURAL STUDIES will publish articles on those practices, texts and cultural domains within which the various social groups that constitute a late capitalist society negotiate patterns of power and meaning. It will engage with the interplay between the personal and the political, between strategies of domination and resistance, between meaning systems and social systems.

CULTURAL STUDIES will seek to develop and transform those perspectives which have traditionally informed the field — structuralism and semiotics, Marxism, psychoanalysis and feminism. Theories of discourse, of power, of pleasure and of the institutionalization of meaning are crucial to its enterprise; so too are those which stress the ethnography of culture.

Contributions should be sent to either the General Editor or one of the Associate Editors. They should be in duplicate and should conform to the Harvard reference system set out in the Notes for Contributors available from members of the Editorial Collective. They may take the form of articles of about 5000 words, of kites (short, provocative or exploratory pieces) of about 2000 words, or of reviews of books, other cultural texts or events.

Advertisements: Enquiries to David Polley, Methuen & Co Ltd, 11 New Fetter Lane, London EC4P 4EE.

Subscription Rates (calendar year only): UK and the rest of the world: individuals £18.00; institutions £35.00; single copies £6.95. North America: individuals $35.00; institutions $55.00; single copies $14.00. All rates include postage; airmail rates on application. Subscriptions to: Subscriptions Department, Methuen & Co Ltd, North Way, Andover, Hants, SP1O 5BE.

Subscribing to *Cultural Studies* in the USA: payments in US dollars may be sent to Associated Book Publishers' account in New York: Account No. 051–70 700–4 at Barclays Bank (New York) Ltd, 300 Park Avenue, New York, NY 10022

ISSN 0950–2386

Transferred to Digital Printing 2004

Advertisement: Enquiries to David Polley, Methuen & Co Ltd, 11 New
Fetter Lane, London EC4P 4EE

CONTENTS

· ARTICLES ·

IAIN CHAMBERS

MAPS FOR THE METROPOLIS: A POSSIBLE GUIDE TO THE PRESENT

> Aron said, pointing to his glass: 'You see, my dear fellow, if you are a phenomenologist, you can talk about this cocktail and make philosophy of it!' Sartre turned pale with emotion at this. Here was just the thing he had been looking to achieve for years.[1]

> Writing isn't to do with signifying, but with surveying, mapping – even of worlds yet to come.[2]

Velo-city

T he French critic Paul Virilio has suggested that the cities of the future will be airports: transit points connecting the movement of millions in flight between one megasuburb and another.[3] That future, of course, has already arrived, and in the most appropriate location: in Texas, midway between Fort Worth and Dallas. The city of J. R. Ewing and amber-glass skyscrapers tested to withstand tornado winds of 150 miles an hour opened its international airport in 1978; a year later it was the third busiest in the world. This back-projection of the future is the world of postmodernism, where everything is 'larger than life', where the referents are swept away by the signs, where the artificial is more 'real' than the real, where Dallas is *Dallas*; where the world is first doubled and then dislocated.

The modern airport, with its shopping malls, restaurants, phones, post office, video games, bars and television chairs, banks and security guards, is a miniaturized city, a simulated metropolis: a metaphor of cosmopolitan existence where the pleasure of travel is not only to arrive, but also not to be in any particular place: to be simultaneously everywhere.

It is a condition typical not only of the contemporary traveller, but also of many a contemporary intellectual. Viewed from 35,000 feet, the world becomes a map. Recently some of the views brought back from high flying have arrived at the conclusion that the world is indeed a map. At that height it is possible to draw connections over great distances, ignoring local obstacles and conditions. At that height certain commonsense objections ('down-to-earth' views) to a reading of the terrain can be ignored. When further height is gained, the flight plan only needs to consider the relation between the plane (undergoing rapid metamorphosis into a spaceship at this point) and the flat referent beneath its fuselage. At this point, the meanings of events elsewhere are incapable of penetrating the space we have put between ourselves and them. Meaning contracts into the pressurized cabin. Life inside the plane, with the observations it affords, becomes more 'real' than the 'reality' we presume to observe. Knowledge of the social, political and cultural globe becomes the knowledge of a second-order reality, a 'simulacrum'.

Flight: to fly, but also to flee. For there also remain more stubborn referents – material, sometimes even geological – that periodically pierce the daily networks of sense: violence, riots, strikes, war, earthquakes, famine, volcanoes, radiation, death. Temporarily connected to the media, the adjectives these events generate hang in the air, symptoms of vital connections: fear, hope, anger, joy, sadness, jubilation, despair. Close up, the world acquires alarming details, a startling complexity.

Meanwhile, between these terrestrial and extraterrestrial co-ordinates, we invariably find ourselves in the immediacy of the contemporary city, inhabiting commercial soundscapes and visualscapes that we personalize, customize and make our own. Here is a world where adverts quote videoclips and videoclips are adverts . . . or . . . are they art? It is a world in which Robert Elms, hip pop pundit and prophet of the fashionable metropolitan youth magazine, *The Face*, can inform the readership of the *Sunday Times* that 'nobody is a teenager any more because everybody is'.[4] In the face of fashion we are all stripped of our histories and turned into 'absolute beginners'.

The idea of 'revival', so central to the cyclical novelty of clothing and contemporary imagery, has nothing to do with history. A revival does not set out to rediscover or faithfully quote a historical moment; rather, it revisits, recycles, re-presents a particular look, a sartorial gesture that has become part of the timeless wardrobe of contemporary mythology. Fashion is ultimately an abstract art. The German sociologist Georg Simmel noted in 1895 that fashion eschews the utilitarian laws of practical clothing for the daring translation of the fragile aesthetics of the novel into a temporary tendency, a style.[5] Hence its fatal fascination: the genesis of fashion rests on rapid decay and precocious death.

In this apparently rootless world, where accelerating signifiers refuse to slow down and be interpreted, we experience the semiotic blur and limitless cross-referencing of a vast urban catalogue. When Harrods department store in London recently opened a new boutique – 'The Way In' – and advertised it in the magazine *i-D* (the 'Worldwide Manual of

THE FACE

IBIZA: HOLIDAY BABYLON
ANIMAL NIGHTS ON FANTASY ISLAND

HOLLYWOOD OR BUST
CELLULOID DREAMS OF THE SOHO TEENS

Style'), the caption consisted of a quote from Roland Barthes on the ontology of the photographic image.

Among these signs and sensations, contemporary popular culture (music, fashion, television, videos, drinking, dancing, clubbing) forms part of a language that provides the architecture of our daily lives and yet is without any apparent purpose. It is a language that exists beyond the obvious pragmatics of the sign; it carries its referents within itself, and encourages the vertiginous experience of the pleasure-in-itself.

However, if we put some critical distance between ourselves and these immediate experiences of the everyday world (the metaphor of the plane returns), then all this can be viewed from another perspective. This language, this culture, these images, these sounds, have a brutal purpose: to make money and reproduce the situations that permit that exercise. And today we have arrived at such a level of cultural commodification that the duplicity of the sign, i.e. that the product might actually 'mean' something, can be done away with. Capitalism, commodification and culture have become one. The 'spectacle' of consumerism, to use Jean Baudrillard's words, has been replaced by the 'obscenity' of an 'excessive transparency'.[6] Contemporary popular culture is merely a seductive sign-play that has arrived at the final referent: the black hole of meaninglessness.

Well, this gives us two views. One is brought back from a height where the air is thin and a distanced, synthetic view is permitted (synthesis (a whole, a totality) = synthetic (artifice, falseness)). The other comes from the altogether more messy and immediate prospects of life on the ground, where an excess of sense, sensations and signs overflows previous limits (intellectual, philosophical, aesthetic, social, political) in a barely recognized complexity. Flying, in more senses than one, is a 'trip', involving a shift in both geographical and existential co-ordinates; we go to an 'other' place, but eventually we also go home. The journey acquires its final shape and sense only once we have returned to the familiar textures of our world.

But I also want to argue that these intellectual flights, such as the journey into the theoretical stratosphere of postmodernism, are important. They provide the possibility for reorientating ourselves, the possibility of recognizing new landmarks and new lines that have been drawn across the map of the contemporary world. A critical intelligence adequate to the fluid complexity of the present is forced to fly regularly. But the importance of such a privileged observation (intellectual, philosophical, aesthetical) is realized only when the global is linked back to the local, when extensive tendencies are embodied in immediate trajectories, when perspectives become tangible projects, when a freedom of vision is translated into a democratization of everyday life.

In the rest of this article I shall try to indicate some of the spaces and fruitful tensions between these two views, between the perspectives of postmodernism and the prospects of popular culture, largely using pop music and its immediate cultures as my guide. I am interested in seeing not only how each plays off the other, but also how postmodernism, whatever form its own intellectualizing might take, has been fundamentally

WORLDWIDE MANUAL OF STYLE

THE i-SPY ISSUE

THE INDISPENSABLE DOCUMENT OF FASHION, STYLE & IDEAS.

anticipated in the metropolitan cultures of the last twenty years: among the electronic signifiers of cinema, television and video, in recording studios and record players, in fashion and youth styles, in all those sounds, images and diverse histories that are daily mixed, recycled and 'scratched' together on that giant screen which is the contemporary city.

This is also to propose a further consequence: that contemporary intellectual work requires not prophets but the more modest labour of 'cultural operators'. Some seek to 'resolve' the world, to explain it away: perhaps it is more significant simply to try to point in certain directions, to suggest certain connections that can be made in the slipstream of a world whose complexity has first to be appreciated if it is going to be better inhabited. So, if postmodernism presumes to provide a shooting script for interpreting the spectacle of the contemporary world, let's try following it on the ground and run its perspectives across the grain of local details, where we can hear the voices of historical subjects making sense of their conditions, exploring their present, constructing a sense of the possible within the limits (and potentials) of their lives.

The look

In Britain, the fashioning of musics into local sense has frequently taken place through the public spectacle of youth and subcultural styles. These confront us with a complex sign-play. Over the surfaces of urban commercial culture they have affected what Dick Hebdige has recently characterized as the 'theology of the look', the world of the conditional tense, the 'as if . . .' world of advertising. It is a world at one remove from daily routines, where our clothes, our bodies, our faces become quotations drawn from the other, imaginary, side of life: from fashion, the cinema, advertising and the infinite suggestions of metropolitan iconography.

Let's take these signs at face value rather than pretend to unveil a 'truth', as though they were merely masks. Perhaps the truth lies in the spaces between the signs, in the multiple interfaces that co-ordinate their movement.

In one sense, all British subcultures have represented stylistic replies to the question of class; a way of responding to one's social condition at the level of the imaginary. But we could add that they therefore also represent a cultural 'exile', an attempt to go beyond the immediacy of class referents and their obvious social contexts. To imitate the slouch of a Hollywood gangster or the pout of his girlfriend was temporarily to extract yourself from the dead weight of your own past. Through the play of style and a sophisticated semiology of goods, subcultures and youth styles in general have tended to separate the idea of social imagery from the world of daily labour and an obvious class position, in the process adding a further dimension to immediate realities.

But things have changed since the heyday of teddy boys, mods and rockers. Other stories have emerged, further margins and more malleable styles have been revealed. The centrality of subcultures to the arguments of

May 24 - 30 190 60p

STILL ONLY 60p!

CITY LIMITS

A-Z
LONDON

P O P V I D E O
HYPE INTO ART?

exclusion, urban romanticism and stylistic contestation has been displaced and dispersed.

In the second half of the 1970s, punk presented us with the breakdown of the image and the dispersal of obvious referents. As the last of historical male subcultures, the summation of previous spectacular styles, punk offered a subculture constructed on the crisis between sign and sense, between culture and class, between style and social situation; its own iconography was perversely constructed on the crisis of the very idea of subculture. The very signs of class, crisis, subculture and sex were ironically re-presented and recycled. But, while this bricolage of popular icons owed something to the New York art world example of Andy Warhol and The Factory, the sign-play here folded in upon itself and swapped a wider sense for a more secluded semantics. Indebted, at least in spirit, to French Dadaist and Situationist leanings (those slogans daubed across the clothes, those 'situations': puking in airport lounges, swearing on television and subsequently hitting the headlines), the codes of punk communicated the choice of avoiding an obvious sense or ready comprehension.

Previous subcultures were dragged out of the closet and irreverently thrown into the window of style. There they were mixed up and perversely confused, without any respect for their earlier sense. The same discourse applied to the music. Like all subcultural music, it was the rude messenger of cultural insolence; but this time around it was also the self-conscious sum of all previous rebellious sounds: the white noise of sonorial anarchy.

With punk – a subculture made up of the bits and pieces of previous subcultural worlds, earlier local totalities – we seemingly stand on the threshold of a new history, that of post-subcultural styles. The firm referents that guided the teddy boys or the mods in their stylistic options in music and clothes are apparently no longer available. Only the skinhead – recalling a mythically 'authentic' reality: the hard, masculine world of the proletariat that is mirrored in his braces, boots, shaved head and tattoos – remains as a stubborn referent, a symbol of the simple, timeless truths, those of the nation, of race, of patriarchy, of class.

Elsewhere, it is collage dressing and musical eclecticism that has dominated the 1980s. Where subcultures once offered a 'strong' sense of singular opposition to the status quo, this has now been replaced by a 'weak' sense of detailed differences; the 'Other' becomes simply the 'others'.

So, in the epoch of the 'post-', even subcultures take their place in the museum of fixed symbolic structures. Involved in metropolitan languages that intersect on the surfaces of the everyday, in London as in Los Angeles, in Naples as in New York, previous rules give way to the flexibility of a collage, to the less traditional, less historicized, hence 'lighter' and more open, prospects of mixing the already seen, the already worn, the already played, the already heard.

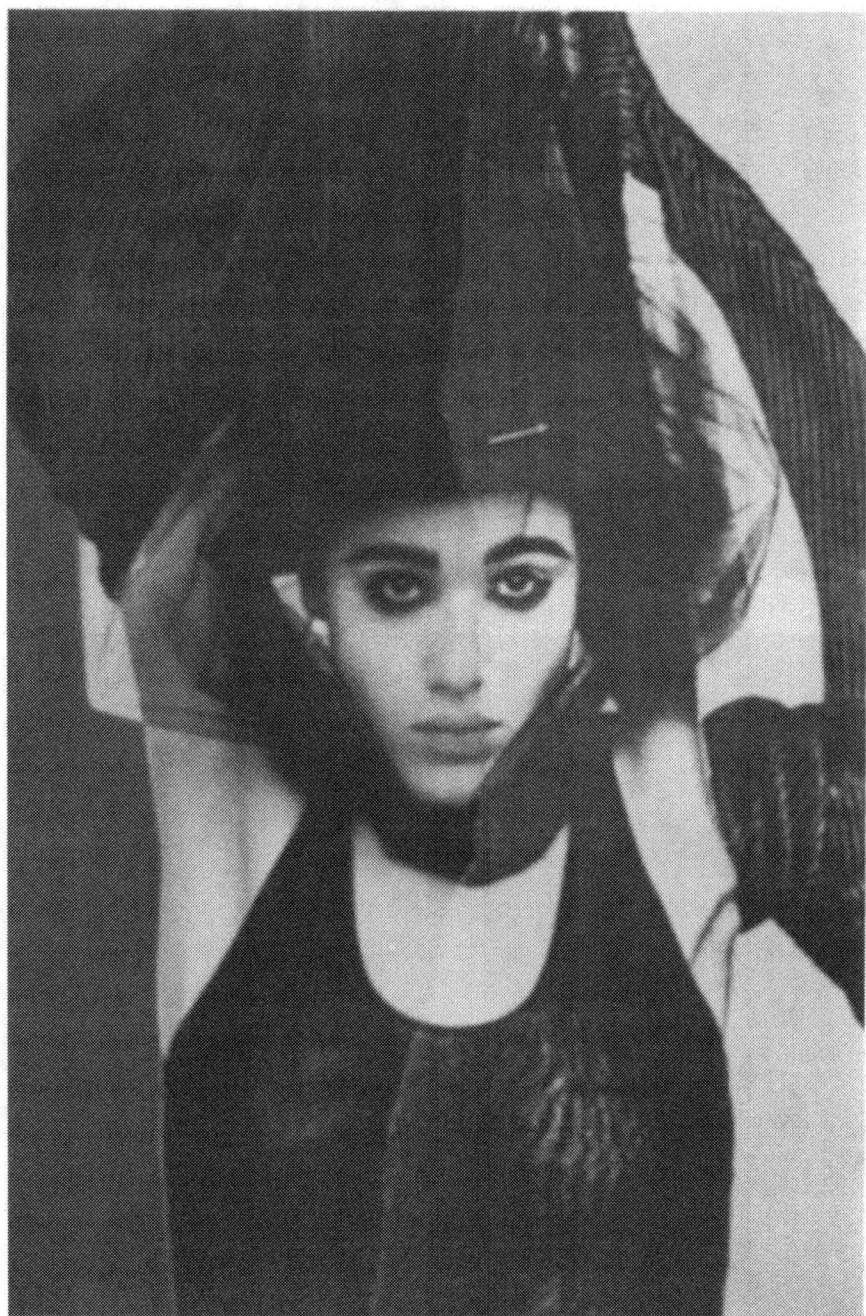

Bodies

Our bodies – dressed, undressed, disguised, accentuated, in movement, in pose – provide another temporary map on which to observe how the signs and histories of style, social position, sexuality and race traverse a surface in common. The body is, in fact, central to pop's semantic universe (and to contemporary urban culture in general). Around, across and through the body the social, cultural and sexual sense of pop music is most intensely organized.

It is above all in the voice, in dance, and in the sartorial regimes that orbit around its sounds that pop music encounters the socialized intimacy of the body. Here there is a public space, elsewhere rarely so easily available, where a whole series of choices – stylistic, sexual and social – are entertained.

All these choices are invariably still dominated by the male principle. Innovations have invariably been in male style, male sexuality and what is socially permissible for men. The use of the falsetto voice, the slight decentring of the phallic code, particularly in the dispersive corporeal rhythms of disco embraced by gay culture, and subsequent gender-bending, although all suggesting different forms of sexuality, rarely involve a relinquishing of male power, of a male order.

However, in the context of playing with the signs of your sex, playing with your 'self', women have also begun to cut up their own image, rearranging the subsequent bits in a more assertive pattern. The process of being looked at – object of the male gaze – grows increasingly complex as women propose themselves as social subjects and the 'look' itself becomes more autonomous, not necessarily tied to male desires, and finds its own powers.

The signs of the 1970s return to be recycled in the daily pragmatics of a post-feminist landscape. From the calculated bravado of Madonna to the poised urban black female beat and iconography of Nona Hendryx, the previous 'ghosts in the hit machine'[7] are perhaps beginning to occupy the sounds, signs, styles and streets of a previous male empire.

Skin, rhythms and roots

Then there is that other world that has persistently accompanied white British subcultures and musical preferences, that cultural 'Other' and loaded metaphor of sought-after difference represented by the style and sounds of black urban culture: Afro-American, Afro-Caribbean and Afro-Hispanic. Initially offering a stylistic referent for Britain's own 'white Negroes', in particular the mods and the later clubland white soul boys, black musics and culture have since the 1960s been transferred from an imaginary American metropolis to becoming a permanent part of British urban culture.

From ska 'rude boys' and reggae rebels to riots, British rap and break crews, black culture, once consigned to the after-hours of public life and

official recognition, now insists on its own particular presence. For, today, being black and living in Britain also involves being British.

A previous response to the cold currents of British life and racial discrimination had been that of withdrawal into the autonomous black universe of Rastafarianism, with the Rastas displaying the stigmata of their exile in 'Babylon' in their woolly tams, I-tal food, ganja and reggae. The popularity of Bob Marley was particularly important in introducing this option to black Britons in the mid-1970s.

Since then, however, living on unemployment benefit and increasingly consigned to a semi-permanent lumpenproletariat, sections of black youth have been directly involved in a move from a self-imposed obscurity to an angry presence. This has been accompanied by younger blacks abandoning the imaginary solution of Rastafarianism and voicing the fact that they have no intention of going anywhere, whether back to Jamaica or on to Ethiopia.

Today, black Britons are increasingly changing into Italian tracksuits and, following the metropolitan strategies of the New York B-Boys, are beginning to mix electric sounds with British realities, translating the mixed-ethnic traditions of a once colonial and colonized subject into local forms. The different 'roots' are transformed into immediate realities. Smiley Culture, from Clapham in South London, is a 'lyrics designer' who has provided one vinyl example of translation between being British and being black ('Cockney Translation'); in the clubs, among the toasters, dubbers and master-mixers, there are many others.

In the heart of the beast: a bestiary of powers

I now want to locate these signs of cultural difference in the wider frame in which the politics of pop (and popular culture) is usually discussed: that of the relationship between the record industry and the music, between the machinery of capital, commerce and industry and ART or CULTURE.

The history of pop music is above all a history of recorded sound. Pop music emerges with the technology of the modern city and the spread of urban culture. Its history – from song sheets and records, through radio and cinema to television and video – is the history of commercially available, reproducible sounds. Pop music and popular culture are made of these circumstances.

This suggests that any attempt to draw a neat distinction between pop music and the record industry, between sounds which we might want to consider as expressions of culture, authenticity and art, on the one hand, and commerce, capital and corruption, on the other, is highly artificial. It involves applying an idealistic and romantic distinction between the 'TRUE' and the 'FALSE', where the 'TRUE' doesn't exist and it is the 'FALSE' that constitutes everyday reality. Such sharp divisions may well allow us to denounce the music industry while *we* maintain a critical distance and intellectual integrity, but I don't feel that it really connects to the specific nature of pop music and popular culture. There is, as Walter Benjamin put it many decades ago, no protective 'aura' surrounding the reproducible artefact.[8] It is there, caught up in the cross-currents of the contemporary world, its production blatantly linked to such circumstances.

So, if we are all inside the machine, if the record industry and commerce are an integral part of contemporary popular music and culture, what sort of aesthetics, politics and sense can be drawn from this situation?

The removal of the simple culture/industry dichotomy suggests that the struggle for sense occurs *inside* a common, although complexly determined, field; not so much between commerce and music, but *inside* the powers of the field they mutually construct. Therefore, the histories and the social signs produced by the encounter of these diverse powers are inhabited; and they are inhabited from the inside. It is from the inside that they are occupied, inflected, deconstructed and reconstructed; that they are appropriated. It is there in the immediate mishmash of the everyday, and not elsewhere, that a sense emerges. For example, Bruce Springsteen as America's favourite son – the romantic 'street boy', the poet as car mechanic – is as much an image for CBS marketing, industrial footwear, Levi-Strauss jeans and a complacent 'Americanicity' as he is for the other side of the 'American Dream' represented by sweat, pathos and muscular liberalism. That is, the public 'he' – the image, the sign, the voice croaking in the dark – is crossed by multiple concerns that are simultaneously open to various senses. The eventual semantics involved here are neither singular nor ultimately free-floating. They are formed in the perpetual struggle between what is available, what seems possible, and the eventual mixture and choices that manage to emerge in particular moments and specific situations.

The payback

Now all these considerations can also be said to represent an important cutting edge in the more usual discussions of the 'political', where cultural details are usually relegated to an instrumental footnote in the discourse. As Andreas Huyssen has recently observed, much politics is but another expression of modernism's underlying hostility to popular or mass culture.[9] If that is the case, and I believe it is, then it seems that the narrow logic of the 'political' has to be rewritten and rearticulated by, to borrow a phrase from American architectural theory, 'learning from popular culture'.[10]

This leads to an expanded sense of complexity, one that breaks with a belief in a unique political or cultural project. The Italian philosopher Gianni Vattimo rightly notes, quoting Walter Benjamin's 'Theses on the philosophy of history', that it is only from the point of view of the 'history of the victors that history is a unitary process in which there is consequentiality and rationality'.[11] The defeated don't see or feel it like this.

It is the winners who write the story, conserving only those parts that can participate in legitimating their power. More immediate and irregular sets

of experiences are violently expelled from the account. Feminism in particular, and the political, cultural and epistemological realignment it has forced across the whole field of social experience and knowledge, has most sharply revealed the edges and limits of that hegemony. To reintroduce the uneven and fragmented experiences of the once obscured, hidden and defeated does mean to reject a homogeneous and unitary sense of culture and politics, of history.

For behind all the talk of commerce and corruption and the subsequent intellectual distaste for popular culture we discover a deeper drama. A certain intellectual formation is discovering that it is losing its grip on the world. The traditional semantic chains that once tied 'truth' and 'meaning' to the powers of an intellectual priesthood and their exclusive institutions (the academy, the university, the scholarly journal, academic publishing) are snapping under the expansion of the contemporary world and the invasion of our experiences by the heterogeneous, the incommensurable, the diverse, the different. It is a world which is no longer automatically white, male or Anglocentric. As a minimum this involves the recognition of a more democratic currency and the acknowledgement that 'the metaphysical adventure is over';[12] that the world cannot be measured against an abstract mean, that critical distance has to dissolve into the networks of critical involvement.

The intellectual can no longer be considered as a dispenser of the Law and Authority, the Romantic poet-priest-prophet, but is rather a humble detective, living, like all of us, under authority and the law, inside the contemporary metropolis that is the modern world. The 'truth' – the intellectual and political authenticity of the moment – is no longer the object of a theoretical imperialism, to be sought and subsequently seized, but becomes rather the horizon in front of which we all more modestly and self-consciously operate.

University of Naples, Italy.

Notes

Some of the prospects set out here were first formulated in a paper given at the symposium 'Music and Society: The Shaping of Contemporary Taste', held at the University of Milwaukee, 3–5 April 1986. I should like to thank the Center for Twentieth Century Studies for giving me the opportunity to present them.

1 Simone de Beauvoir, *The Prime of Life* (Harmondsworth: Penguin, 1966), p. 135.
2 Gilles Deleuze and Félix Guattari, 'Rhizome', *Ideology and Consciousness*, 8 (1981), p. 51.
3 P. Virilio and S. Lotringer, *Pure War* (New York: Semiotext(e), 1983).
4 Robert Elms, 'Time to wake up from the teen dream', *Sunday Times*, 12 January 1986, p. 37.
5 Georg Simmel, *La moda* (Rome: Riuniti, 1985).

6 Jean Baudrillard, 'The ecstasy of communication', in H. Foster (ed.), *Postmodern Culture* (London: Pluto Press, 1985), pp. 130–3.

7 S. Steward and S. Garrett, *Signed, Sealed and Delivered: True Life Stories of Women in Pop* (London: Pluto Press, 1985; Boston, Mass.: South End Press, 1985), p. 7.

8 Walter Benjamin, 'The work of art in the age of mechanical reproduction', in *Illuminations* (London: Fontana, 1973), pp. 219–53.

9 Andreas Huyssen, 'Mapping the postmodern', *New German Critique*, 33 (Fall 1984), pp. 11–52.

10 Robert Ventura, Denise Scott Brown, Steven Izenour, *Learning from Las Vegas* (Cambridge, Mass.: MIT Press, 1977).

11 Gianni Vattimo, 'Dialettica, differenza, pensiero debole', in G. Vattimo and P. A. Rovatti (eds), *Il pensiero debole* (Milan: Feltrinelli, 1983), p. 15.

12 G. Vattimo and P. A. Rovatti, 'Premessa', in Vattimo and Rovatti (eds), *Il pensiero debole*, p. 9.

The author wishes to thank the following for the use of photographs: Tony Viramontes/ *The Face*, Eamonn McCabe/*i-D* Magazine, Derek Ridgers, *City Limits*. Other photographs are by Iain Chambers.

NICHOLAS GARNHAM

CONCEPTS OF CULTURE: PUBLIC POLICY AND THE CULTURAL INDUSTRIES

Nicholas Garnham's *Concepts of Culture* is an important document, not only for its internal positions and arguments, but also because of the context of its own production. It was written originally for a conference on the cultural industries in London, in December 1983, and published as a pamphlet by the Greater London Council (GLC). The immediate impetus to put the cultural industries on the political agenda of local government in London was the build-up of activity within both central government and private industry around plans for the introduction of cable television. The GLC was determined not to be reduced to a merely reactive position on this issue, but, once confronted, the question of what a cable policy might look like raised much larger questions.

The Labour administration of the GLC under Ken Livingstone was attempting to construct an alternative to the top-down, national approach to economic strategy which, among other things, traditionally left the formulation of cultural policy to central government. The GLC wanted to develop, within the limitations of its power and resources, a strategy that combined popular planning with job creation. At the economic level, such cultural industries as publishing, music, television, film, newspapers, advertising and, to a lesser extent, information technology are concentrated in London, despite their national reach and significance. The need for economic planning in these sectors was paralleled by the GLC's policy, under Tony Banks, to move away from traditional definitions of culture as a site of individual excellence and 'Art', towards a redefinition which focused on popular culture and media. *Concepts of Culture* was a contribution to this work of policy reformulation, and even within the labour movement it was (and is) a challenging piece. Both traditional Labour and left Labour positions were, historically, suspicious of 'the Market', and they weren't exempt from élitist assumptions about culture either.

Thus *Concepts of Culture* was a decisive intervention into both public policy-making and left politics. Culture was henceforth on the political agenda of the GLC, and its redefinition around the notion of the popular cultural industries led to numerous initiatives in which GLC support was redirected – for instance, towards financial support for the 'indies' (independent record labels), football clubs, and the independent film and video sector, along with myriad community, grass-roots and issue-based organizations.

We reprint *Concepts of Culture* here, then, in recognition of the need for cultural studies to engage not only with cultural forms and practices but also with economic strategies and market forces. Despite the abolition of the GLC by the Conservative government in 1986, the work inaugurated by *Concepts of Culture* has continued. Cultural analysis and policy-making, together with material support for cultural industries, is now within the province of the Cultural

Industries Division of the Greater London Enterprise Board (GLEB). This body is carrying forward the work of the Economic Policy Group of the GLC which produced, apart from *Concepts of Culture* itself, reports on all the major media industries in London. Readers may wish to know that Geoff Mulgan and Ken Worpole of GLEB are working together on a book about the whole project, and that the GLC itself published a book, *The State of the Art or the Art of the State: Strategies of the Cultural Industries in London*, which gathered much of this material together.

John Hartley

T o mobilize the concept of the cultural industries as central to an analysis of cultural activity and of public cultural policy is to take a stand against a whole tradition of idealist cultural analysis. This tradition, well delineated in the British form, for instance, by Raymond Williams in *Culture and Society*, defines culture as a realm separate from, and often actively opposed to, the realm of material production and economic activity.

This is important for our present purposes because, in general, public cultural policies have evolved from within that tradition. Public intervention, in the form of subsidy, is justified on the grounds (1) that culture possesses inherent values, of life enhancement or whatever, which are fundamentally opposed to and in danger of damage by commercial forces; (2) that the need for these values is universal, uncontaminated by questions of class, gender and ethnic origin; and (3) that the market cannot satisfy this need.

A further crucial component of this ideology is the special and central status attributed to the 'creative artist' whose aspirations and values, seen as stemming from some unfathomable and unquestionable source of genius, inspiration or talent, are the source of cultural value. The result of placing artists at the centre of the cultural universe has not been to shower them with gold, for artistic poverty is itself an ideologically potent element in this view of culture, but to define the policy problem as one of finding audiences for their work, rather than vice versa. When audiences cannot be found, at least at a price and in a quantity which will support the creative activity, the market is blamed and the gap is filled by subsidy.

It is important to note that most of those on the left who have challenged this dominant view of culture as élitist have themselves tacitly if not explicitly accepted the remaining assumptions of the tradition they were rejecting. Indeed, in my view this in part accounts for their limited success in shifting the terms of the policy debate and the effortless ease with which they have been incorporated.

One result of this cultural policy-making tradition has been to marginalize public intervention in the cultural sphere and to make it purely reactive to processes which it cannot grasp or attempt to control. For, while this tradition has been rejecting the market, most people's cultural needs and aspirations are being, for better or worse, supplied by the market as goods and services. If one turns one's back on an analysis of that dominant cultural process, one cannot understand either the culture of our time or the challenges and opportunities which that dominant culture offers to public policy makers.

We can get some idea of the relative orders of magnitude between public-sector expenditure on cultural activity and private, market expenditure if we compare the £673.8 million of public expenditure on libraries, museums and galleries and other cultural activities in the United Kingdom in 1981–2 (see table 1) with the £15,538 million of 1982 consumer expenditure on recreation, entertainment and education (see table 2) and with the total media advertising expenditure in 1982 of £3216 million (see table 4).

Table 1 Public cultural expenditure in the UK, 1981–1982 (£ million)

	Central government	Local authorities	Total
Libraries	39.1	320.5	359.6
Museums and galleries	76.3	60.7	137.0
Other cultural facilities	97.6	79.6	177.2
Total	213.0	460.8	673.8

Note: There is a high proportion devoted to libraries, particularly for local authority expenditure. It is worth noting that Greater London spent nearly five times as much per head of the population on cultural facilities other than museums and galleries as any other region in Britain. Of this figure of £496 per head in 1981–2, £336 was spent by the boroughs and £133 by the GLC.

An analysis of culture structured around the concept of the cultural industries, on the other hand, directs our attention precisely at the dominant private market sector. It sees culture, defined as the production and circulation of symbolic meaning, as a material process of production and exchange, part of, and in significant ways determined by, the wider economic processes of society with which it shares many common features.

Thus, as a descriptive term, 'cultural industries' refers to those institutions in our society which employ the characteristic modes of production and organization of industrial corporations to produce and disseminate symbols in the form of cultural goods and services, generally, although not exclusively, as commodities. These include newspapers, periodical and book publishing, record companies, music publishers, commercial sports organizations, etc. In all these cultural processes, we characteristically find at some point the use of capital-intensive, techno-logical means of mass production and/or distribution, highly developed divisions of labour and hierarchical modes of managerial organization, with the goal, if not of profit maximization, at least of efficiency. I refer to this as a descriptive use of the term 'cultural industries' because it describes characteristics common to the cultural process in all industrial societies, whether capitalist or socialist. Within the descriptive usage we need to note a further distinction made by Adorno, who originally coined the term, between those cultural industries which employ industrial technology and modes of organization to produce and distribute cultural goods or services which are themselves produced by largely traditional or pre-industrial means (e.g. books and records) and those where the cultural form itself is industrial (e.g. newspapers, films and TV programmes). We need to remember this distinction because the two forms tend to give rise to different relations of production and types of economic organization.

But the term 'cultural industries' can also be used analytically to focus upon the effects on the cultural process within the capitalist mode of production of cultural goods and services produced and distributed as commodities by labour, which is itself a commodity.

A key point here is that the cultural sector operates as an integrated economic whole because industries and companies within it compete:

1 for a limited pool of disposable consumer income;
2 for a limited pool of advertising revenue;
3 for a limited amount of consumption time;
4 for skilled labour.

Consumers' expenditure

Consumer expenditure on cultural goods and services has been rising slowly as a proportion of total expenditure, as consumption of basic essentials, such as food and clothing, reaches saturation point. However, this movement has been within limits, and studies have shown this expenditure to be inelastic not only in general but also in the sense that for individuals and families expenditure does not rise in line with income. This is probably linked to the question of limited consumption time.

Advertising expenditure

Table 4 shows the close relationship between total advertising expenditure and both consumer expenditure and GNP. Since 1952 it has varied between 1.94 and 1.15 per cent of consumer expenditure, and between 1.43 and 0.89 per cent of GNP. Moreover, in real terms, total advertising expenditure has remained remarkably stable, growing over the last twenty years by only £431 million and remaining virtually static from 1964 to 1976. Against a background of a high level of advertising in the UK in relation to GNP compared with other European economies, the limits of the advertising revenue pool are plain.

Table 2   Consumer expenditure on recreation, entertainment and education in the UK, 1982 (£ million)

	1982	At 1980 prices		
		1980	1981	1982
Radio, TV and other durable goods	2,161.	1,567	1,798	2,200
TV and video hire charges, licence fees and repairs	1,997	1,571	1,640	1,758
Sports goods, toys, games and camping equipment	1,304	1,211	1,153	1,163
Other recreational goods	2,700	2,288	2,328	2,504
Betting and gaming	1,832	1,572	1,496	1,462
Other recreational and entertainment services	1,608	1,396	1,294	1,198
Books, newspapers and magazines	2,396	1,856	1,805	1,729
Education	1,540	1,092	1,145	1,186
Total	15,538	12,553	12,659	13,200

Source: National Income and Expenditure
Note: This illustrates both the dramatic rise in the expenditure on domestic hardware and the high proportion that the buying, renting and servicing of such hardware, together with TV licence payments, occupies in total consumer leisure expenditure – approximately 25 per cent. These figures illustrate the trend for cultural consumption to withdraw into the home via a range of technological delivery systems focused especially around the TV set. This, of course, parallels TV viewing figures as a percentage of cultural consumption time.

Table 3   Average weekly household expenditure in GLC areas compared to the UK as a whole, 1981 (£)

	GLC	UK
TV, radio, musical instruments and cine repair	2.87	1.82
Books, magazines, newspapers and periodicals	2.13	2.01
Cinema	0.31	0.14
Theatres, sporting events and other entertainment	1.19	1.05
TV licence and rental	1.20	1.44

Note: There is higher spending on all categories except TV licence and rental, which is reflected in the marginally lower percentages of households with TV: 95.1 per cent in the GLC compared with 96.7 per cent for the UK in 1980–1. The higher levels of cultural expenditure in London in turn reflect higher average levels of household income, £193.47 for the GLC as opposed to £167.60 for the UK as a whole.

Table 4 Total advertising expenditure and its relation to consumer expenditure and gross national product, 1952–1982

Year	Total expenditure in 1975 prices[a] (£ million)	Total expenditure in current prices (£ million)	Total expenditure as a percentage of	
			Consumer expenditure[b]	Gross national product[b]
1952	NA	123	1.15	0.89
1956	NA	197	1.43	1.08
1960	NA	323	1.91	1.43
1961	897	338	1.90	1.40
1962	885	348	1.84	1.38
1963	925	371	1.84	1.38
1964	1005	416	1.94	1.42
1965	1002	435	1.90	1.39
1966	991	447	1.84	1.35
1967	976	451	1.77	1.29
1968	1039	503	1.83	1.34
1969	1067	544	1.86	1.37
1970	1022	554	1.74	1.27
1971	997	591	1.66	1.20
1972	1113	708	1.76	1.28
1973	1259	874	1.91	1.36
1974	1118	900	1.72	1.21
1975	967	967	1.50	1.03
1976	1020	1188	1.59	1.07
1977	1110	1499	1.75	1.19
1978	1254	1834	1.86	1.27
1979	1285	2131	1.82	1.27
1980	1306	2555	1.89	1.32
1981	1287	2818	1.88	1.34
1982	1316	3216	NA	NA

Notes
[a] Figures in this column are obtained by deflating the current price figures by the retail price index.
[b] Owing to revisions made by the Central Statistical Office to GNP and consumer expenditure data – often going back many years – the ratios given in this table may differ slightly from ratios given in previous years.

Consumption time

For most people, cultural consumption is confined to a so-called free time, the extension of which is limited by the material necessities of work and sleep. If we assume a working week including travel of 45 hours and sleep time of 48 hours per week, that leaves 75 hours per week in which all other activities have to be fitted. On average, 20 hours per week are taken up by TV viewing.

Cultural consumption is particularly time-consuming in the sense that the most common and popular form of culture, namely narrative and its musical equivalent, are based upon manipulation of time itself, and thus they offer deep resistances to attempts to raise the productivity of consumption time. This scarcity of consumption time explains:

1 the acute competition for audiences in the cultural sector;
2 the tendency to concentrate cultural consumption in the home, thus cutting out travel time;
3 as recent Swedish studies have shown, a sharp rise in the unit cost of each minute of consumption time, in particular as investment on domestic hardware increases while the time for using such hardware does not. Thus in Sweden between 1970 and 1979 time spent listening to music rose by 20 per cent while the cost rose by 86 per cent, with each hour of listening costing 55 per cent more.

The labour market

The various cultural industries compete in the same market for labour. Individual film-makers, writers, musicians or electricians may move in their work from film, to television, to live theatre. The electronic engineer may work in manufacturing or broadcasting. The journalist may work in newspapers, periodicals, radio or television.

This unified labour market is reflected in trade-union organizations. The Association of Cinematograph, Television and Allied Technicians (ACTT) organizes across film, television and radio, the National Union of Journalists (NUJ) across newspapers, books, magazines, radio and television. The Musicians' Union members work in film, radio, television and records as well as live performances, and so on.

As a result of these levels of integration within the cultural sector, a shift in one place affects the structure of the whole sector. The introduction of a new television channel, such as Channel Four, restructures the broadcasting, film and advertising market in specific ways. Even more, of course, will this be the case with cable and satellite services. The introduction of a new colour supplement has repercussions upon the finances of other publications, but may well also have cross-effects on broadcasting revenue. The same holds true for public intervention. One needs to be aware that one may be playing a zero-sum game, and that all options are not simultaneously open.

A classic example of this interaction and of the ways in which the dynamics of the private sector impact on the public sector is the relation between ITV and BBC. Because ITV holds a monopoly of television advertising, and because there has in general been a high demand for this commodity, extra broadcasting hours mean, for ITV, extra revenue, more efficient utilization of plant and thus higher profit. There has therefore been steady pressure from ITV, in common with commercial broadcasting systems throughout the world, to expand the hours of broadcasting – pressure which has been successful. For the BBC, on the other hand, expansion of hours leads to increases in costs with no increase in revenue. They have, however, been forced to respond to ITV because of the need to compete for audiences, thus increasing the pressure to spend more public money on broadcasting if the balance between public and private sectors is to be maintained.

The structure and dynamics of the cultural industries

The particular economic nature of the cultural industries can be explained in terms of the general tendencies of commodity production within the capitalist mode of production as modified by the special characteristics of the cultural commodity. Thus we find competition driving the search for profits via increased productivity, but it takes specific forms.

There is a contradiction at the heart of the cultural commodity. On the one hand, there is a very marked drive towards expanding the market share or the form this takes in the cultural sector, audiences. This is explained by the fact that in general, because one of the use-values of culture is novelty or difference, there is a constant need to create new products which are all in a sense prototypes. That is to say, the cultural commodity resists that homogenization process which is one of the material results of the abstract equivalence of exchange to which the commodity form aspires. This drive for novelty within cultural production means that in general the costs of reproduction are marginal in relation to the costs of production (the cost of each record pressing is infinitesimal compared to the cost of recording, for instance). Thus the marginal returns from each extra sale tend to grow, leading in turn to a powerful thrust towards audience maximization as the preferred profit maximization strategy.

On the other hand, the cultural commodity is not destroyed in the process of consumption. My reading of a book or watching of a film does not make it any less available to you. Moreover, the products of the past live on and can be relatively easily and cheaply reproduced anew. Thus it has been difficult to establish the scarcity on which price is based. And thus cultural goods (and some services, such as broadcasting, for technical reasons) tend towards the condition of a public good. Indeed, one can observe a marked tendency, where they are not *de jure* so treated, for consumers to so treat them *de facto* through high levels of piracy, as is now the case with records, video cassettes and books. (It should be noted that this in its turn relates to another contradiction in the cultural sphere, on which I shall comment shortly, between the producers of cultural hardware and software. It is the development of a market in cheap reproduction technology that makes piracy so difficult to control.) In contradiction, then, to the drive to maximize audiences, a number of strategies have had to be developed for artificially limiting access in order to create scarcity.

The drive to audience maximization leads to the observed tendency towards a high level of concentration, internationalization and cross-media ownership in the cultural industries. The strategies to limit access have taken a variety of forms:

1 Monopoly or oligopolistic controls over distribution channels, some-times, as in broadcasting, linked to the state. One often finds here a close relationship between commercial interests and those of state control.
2 An attempt to concentrate the accumulation process on the provision of cultural hardware – e.g. radio and television receivers, hi-fi, VCRs, etc. – with the programmes, as in the early days of British broadcasting, as necessary loss-leaders. The rationale for the introduction of cable in the UK is an example of this.
3 The creation of the audience as a commodity for sale to advertisers, where the cultural software merely acts as a free lunch. This has proved itself the most successful solution; both the increased proportion of advertising to sales revenue in the press and periodicals market, culminating in the growth of free newspapers and magazines, and the steady expansion of wholly advertising-financed broadcasting services, are indications of this.
4 The creation of commodities, of which news is the classic example, which require constant reconsumption.

Audiences, cultural repertoire and distribution

The third key characteristic of the cultural commodity lies in the nature of its use-values. These have proved difficult if not impossible to pin down in any precise terms, and demand for them appears to be similarly volatile. As I have already remarked, culture is above all the sphere for the expression of difference. Indeed, some analysts would claim that cultural goods are pure positional goods, their use-value being as markers of social and individual difference. While this aspect of culture merits much deeper and more extended analysis, it is only necessary here to draw one key conclusion, namely that demand for any single cultural product is impossible to predict. Thus the cultural industries, if they are to establish a stable market, are forced to create a relationship with an audience or public to whom they offer not a simple cultural good, but a cultural repertoire across which the risks can be spread. For instance, in the record industry only 1 in 9 singles and 1 in 16 LPs makes a profit, and 3 per cent of the output can account for up to 50 per cent of turnover. Similarly, in films the top 10 films out of 119 in the UK market in 1979 took 32 per cent of the box-office receipts and the top 40 took 80 per cent.

Thus the drive to audience maximization, the need to create artificial scarcity by controlling access and the need for a repertoire bring us to the central point in this analysis. *It is cultural distribution, not cultural production, that is the key locus of power and profit.* It is access to distribution which is the key to cultural plurality. The cultural process is as much, if not more, about creating audiences or publics as it is about producing cultural artefacts and performances. Indeed, that is why that stress upon the cultural producers that I noted earlier is so damaging.

We need to recognize the importance, within the cultural industries and within the cultural process in general, of the function which I shall call, for want of a better word, editorial: the function not just of creating a cultural repertoire matched to a given audience or audiences but at the same time of matching the cost of production of that repertoire to the spending powers of that audience. These functions may be filled by somebody or some institution referred to variously as a publisher, a television channel controller, a film distributor, etc. It is a vital function totally ignored by many cultural analysts, a function as creative as writing a novel or directing a film. It is a function, moreover, which will exist centrally within the cultural process of any geographically dispersed society with complex division of labour.

Taking these various factors into account, we are now in a position to understand why our dominant cultural processes and their modes of organization are the way they are. The newspaper and the television and radio schedule are montages of elements to appeal to as wide a range of readers, viewers and listeners as possible. The high levels of concentration in the international film, record and publishing industries are responses to the problem of repertoire. The dominance of broadcast television stems from its huge efficiency as a distribution medium, with its associated economies of scale.

For this reason, the notion that the new technologies of cable and VCR are fragmenting the market rather than shifting the locus of oligopolistic power needs to be treated with caution, since there are strict limits to how far such fragmentation can go economically.

The hierarchy of cultural industries

As I have noted, power in the cultural sector clusters around distribution, the channel of access to audiences. It is here that we typically find the highest levels of capital intensity, ownership concentration and multi-nationalization, the operation of classic industrial labour processes and relations of production with related forms of trade-union organization. These characteristics are exhibited to their highest degree in the manu-facture of the hardware of cultural distribution, especially domestic hardware. This is a sub-sector increasingly dominated by a few Japanese corporations such as Matsushita, Sony, Sanyo, Toshiba and Hitachi, together with Eastman Kodak, Philips and RCA. The major UK firm of this type is Thorn-EMI.

Then there are the major controllers of channels of software distribution, often closely linked to specific modes of reproduction, such as record pressing or newspaper printing. In non-print media there is again a high level of concentration and internationalization, and US firms dominate, owing to the large size of the domestic US market. Here we find some of the same firms as in hardware, e.g. RCA, Thorn-EMI and Philips joined by firms such as Warner, CBS, Time-Life, Gulf-Western and MCA. The multinationalization of print media has been limited by barriers of language. None the less, apart from the high levels of concentration in the national UK market, with three groups controlling 74 per cent of daily newspaper circulation, two of these groups – News International and Reed International[1] – have extensive foreign interests.

The increasing tendency in this field, as an extension of the principle of repertoire, is the formation of multi-media conglomerates. Examples are Pearson-Longman and Thorn-EMI[2] in the UK, who own interests across a number of media, thus enabling them both to exploit the same product, be it a film, a book or a piece of music, across several media, and also to expand the principles of risk-spreading not only across a range of consumer choice in one medium but also across consumers' entire range of cultural choice. The development of such centres of cultural powers also, of course, raises barriers to entry.

Around these centres of power cluster groups of satellites. These satellites can be either small companies, for instance independent production companies in relation to Channel Four, or individual cultural workers such as freelance journalists, writers, actors and film directors. In these satellite sectors we find high levels of insecurity, low levels of profitability, low levels of unionization and, where they exist, weak trade-union organizations. Often labour is not waged at all, but labour power is rented out for a royalty.

The existence of this dependent satellite sector fulfils a very important function for the cultural industries because it enables them to shift much of the cost and risk of cultural research and development off their own shoulders and on to this exploited sector, some of which is then indeed supported from the public purse. It also enables them to maintain a consistently high turnover of creative cultural labour without running the risk of labour unrest, or bearing the cost of redundancy or pension payments. Their cup brimmeth over when, as is often the case, the workers themselves willingly don this yoke in the name of freedom.

The market and culture

Before turning to the specific problems of London and of public intervention in the cultural sector, one last general analytical question must be raised: what should be our attitude to the relation between the market and the cultural process? There is that general tradition, to which I alluded at the beginning of this paper, which regards culture and the market as inherently inimical. This view is powerfully reinforced within the socialist tradition by opposition to the capitalist mode of production.

I think it is crucial, however, to separate the concept of the market from the concept of the capitalist mode of production, that is to say from a given structure of ownership and from the special features derived from labour as a market commodity. In terms of this relationship between consumers, distributors and producers of cultural goods and services, the market has much to recommend it, provided that consumers enter that market with equal endowments and that concentration of ownership power is reduced, controlled or removed. However, we must be clear that removal of the power vested in private or unaccountable public ownership will not remove the need for the function I have described as editorial, whether such a function is exercised individually or collectively. It also has to be stressed that even within the capitalist mode of production the market has, at crucial historical junctures, acted as a liberating cultural force. One thinks of the creation of both the novel and the newspaper by the rising bourgeoisie in the eighteenth century and of working men's clubs and the working-class seaside holiday in the late nineteenth century.

Indeed, the cultural market, as it has developed in the last 150 years in the UK as a substitute for patronage in all its forms, cannot be read either as a destruction of high culture by vulgar commercialism or as a suppression of authentic working-class culture, but should be read as a complex hegemonic dialectic of liberation and control – which makes an analysis, for instance, of the role of broadcasting and of the BBC public-service tradition so difficult.

What analysis of the cultural industries does bring home to us is the need to take the question of the scarcity and thus of the allocation of cultural resources seriously, together with the question of audiences – who they are, how they are formed and how they can best be served. For it needs to be said that the only alternative to the market which we have constructed, with the partial exception of broadcasting, has tended either simply to subsidize the existing tastes and habits of the better-off or to create a new form of public culture which has no popular audience; cultural workers create for the only audience they know, namely the cultural bureaucrats who pay the bill and upon whom they become psychologically dependent even while reviling them.

The culture industries and London

As a result of the work for the public hearings on cable and the London Industrial Strategy, the Economic Policy Group has identified the cultural sector as a prime site for possible GLC intervention, both because of its intrinsic importance to the London economy and because through the arts and recreation budget the GLC is already making a significant intervention which, if it is to produce the maximum long-term benefit in terms of access to cultural opportunities for Londoners, needs to be planned in the light of the economic dynamic of the cultural sector as a whole.

Because of London's historic role as not only a national but also an imperial capital city, the cultural industries are heavily concentrated in London as the hub of both a national and an international market. Printing and publishing is now London's largest manufacturing sector, employing in 1978 112,300, with book publishers exporting 34 per cent of their output. Electrical engineering, which provides the infrastructure of cultural transmission, is the second largest manufacturing sector, with 99,300.

Between them these two sectors make up one-third of London's manufacturing employment.

A recent EPG study (EC 940) shows that about 50,000 people are employed in London in the broadcasting, film and video industry and that nearly 30 per cent of all UK cinema box-office receipts are taken in Greater London. A further 20,000 are employed in advertising, 59 per cent of the UK total.

The Institute of Employment Research at the University of Warwick estimated in their spring 1982 review of the economy and employment that for 1980–90 the category of literary, artistic and sports production would be the fastest-growing area of employment, increasing nationally by 30 per cent or 132,000.

The cultural industries and public policy

The implications for public cultural policy of the analysis I have outlined above are very much on the international agenda. In April 1980 the Council of Europe held a conference on the state's role *vis-à-vis* the cultural industries and is engaged in continuing work in this field. In 1978 UNESCO approved the implementation of a comparative research programme on cultural industries. As a result, a meeting of experts on 'The place and role of cultural industries in the cultural development of societies' was held in Montreal in June 1980, and this was followed by a World Conference on Cultural Policies in Mexico in July 1982.

The French government has recently set up an investment fund for the cultural industries, aimed both at helping those industries to compete against foreign, especially US, products in the domestic market, and at penetrating export markets.

The recent second report from the UK Government Information Technology Advisory Panel sees software in all its forms as a growing international market which the UK is in a good position to exploit, and it advocates government support, on grounds similar to the French initiative, for the development of what they describe as tradeable information, a category that includes entertainment.

These new approaches to public cultural policy are motivated in part by a realization of the growing economic importance of the cultural sector and in part by the perceived inadequacies of traditional approaches to cultural policy, which at best act as a temporary band-aid of almost total irrelevance to the health of the patient. They are in large part an attempt to prop up a largely nineteenth-century structure of cultural practice, to which the majority of citizens are wholly indifferent.

What, then, should our reaction be? What kind of policy questions do we now need to pose?

1 Debates, organizational energy and finance need to be directed towards broadcasting for two reasons:

(a) Broadcasting is the heartland of contemporary cultural practice because of the high proportion of consumers' time and money devoted to it and because, as a result of that concentration of attention, it is itself both directly and indirectly the major cultural patron. For instance, the BBC spends more per annum supporting cultural workers in the narrow sense of that term, about £105 million more, than the Arts Council. In addition, the success of films, records and books is becoming increasingly dependent upon broadcasting exposure. Indeed, television and radio chat shows, those characteristic contemporary broadcasting forms, are now an integral part of the marketing apparatus of other media.

(b) Broadcasting is now the major form of public intervention in the cultural process. The income of the BBC alone in 1982 was £563.6 million, nearly as large as all other public expenditure on culture, including public libraries and museums. However, if we include the ITV and ILR revenues, which were £820.2 million and £20 million respectively, on the grounds that their expenditure, through the Independent Broadcasting Authority (IBA) and the Channel Four board, is under significant degrees of public control specifically designed to counteract market pressures, however inadequately, then we have some true measure of the weight of broadcasting as a public intervention in our culture. It is, therefore, a high priority both to defend this public sphere from the threats posed to it by current government cable initiatives and to work to make a reality of the possibilities of true public accountability which its existence makes possible.

2 Expenditure on public libraries represents over 50 per cent of all public expenditure on culture and a much higher proportion of local authority expenditure. A large and increasing proportion of that expenditure goes on staff and buildings. It must be sensible to see that maximum use is made of that asset. For instance, perhaps it is libraries that need to become both alternative film and video exhibition venues, distribution channels for cultural goods, marketing centres for cultural services.

3 We need to stop looking at the media in isolation. The public sector too needs to exploit economies of scale and the notion of repertoire. Thus community bookshop initiatives have to be co-ordinated with policies to develop alternative, community-based venues for film and video exhibitions, for the performing arts and for the display of visual arts. Thus the distribution of books, records, periodicals, films and video needs to be analysed as one problem.

4 We need to concentrate our interventions not on production but on distribution in the widest sense. That is, we need to develop public-sector audience research and marketing expertise and ways of placing enhanced cultural choice in the hands of individuals and groups, choices which these distribution services would then enable cultural workers to respond to, perhaps helping them to be more nearly self-sufficient. This seems preferable to the current tendency, which is to encourage the

overproduction of cultural goods and services for which there is no audience.

5 If we are serious about improving access to cultural production for disadvantaged groups such as women and ethnic minorities, then we need to negotiate with the major companies in the cultural industries over their training and recruitment policies in collaboration with the relevant trade unions. But this raises an issue we cannot dodge. No one has the *right* to be a cultural worker. Their numbers will always be limited. The illusion of free access is at present sustained only by the high levels of unemployment and marginal employment. The price that would have to be paid for better terms and conditions is limitation on access. This applies as much to existing publicly funded cultural activities as it does to the private sector. How, then, is such access to be controlled, on what criteria and by whom?

6 Are there certain cultural trends we cannot buck, in particular the trend to concentrate cultural consumption in the home? The GLC has to decide how to respond to the dramatic decline in cinema attendances and the resulting prospect of widespread cinema closure in Greater London. Should those cinemas be taken over and, if so, for what purpose, if cinema-going cannot be re-created? Perhaps resources would be better spent ensuring that the choice people received at home was enhanced.

7 Should we campaign for a cultural levy on advertising? Advertising, for reasons I have outlined, is a crucial and growing source of cultural funding. It is a source of funding which structures cultural production and distribution in specific ways which are not directly responsive to the demands of audiences. In particular it subsidizes more heavily the cultural consumption of the better-off. There is, therefore, a powerful case for adopting on a national and cultural sector-wide basis the strategy adopted within the IBA system, through differential rentals and the Channel Four levy, of redistributing advertising expenditure to support cultural provision which advertising would not support. The problem is to construct appropriate mechanisms to this end.

Polytechnic of Central London.

1 Since this article was written Reed International have sold their newspaper interests to Robert Maxwell.
2 Since this article was written Thorn-EMI have disposed of their media interests. A better example now would be the Robert Maxwell empire.

REGIMES OF TRUTH AND
THE POLITICS OF READING:
A *BLIVIT*

T hese days – the days of *Whoops! Apocalypse*, nukespeak, deconstruction, Rajneeshes, *homo ludens*, Memphis design, Popemobiles, Foucault, Lindy Chamberlain, Wapping, semiotics, remote-control TV – these days it is necessary to start with incommensurables; with things that don't fit.

Perhaps it is appropriate, in these days, that high academic theories, like Popemobiles, scour the terrain of popular culture, searching for truths in the domains of the profane, the commonplace, the demotic. Kurt Vonnegut has coined the term *blivit* for his own combination of incommensurables: an 'all-frequencies assault on the sensibilities' made of 'fiction, drama, history, biography and journalism'. A *blivit*, writes Vonnegut, can be defined as 'two pounds of shit in a one pound bag'.[1] Somewhere in the bag, Vonnegut records his own great-grandfather's belief that truth 'must always be recognized as the paramount requisite of human society'. Vonnegut comments: 'As I myself said in another place, I began to have my doubts about truth after it was dropped on Hiroshima.'[2]

■ ■ ■

In the mass media too, truth matters: it has power to command; it is an instrument of power to be dropped on the unsuspecting. Unlike the theoretical discourses on truth, which can (at least in principle) keep their boundaries pure and uncontaminated by quotidian incident, existential hum or ontological murmur, the media are structurally *blivitous* – the only boundaries that cannot be crashed here are deadlines. Songs, sights, stories and speech are continuously produced and deployed, after the manner of Vonnegut, to combine and intertwine 'the tidal power of a major novel with the bone-rattling immediacy of front-line journalism . . . the flashy enthusiasms of musical theatre, the lethal jab of the short story, the sachet of personal letters, the oompah of American history, and oratory in the bow-wow style'.[3] Such a mixture of genres, rhetorics, referential domains and bodily experiences clearly needs something pretty powerful to keep it all sorted out.

Regimes are conditions under which processes occur, the prevailing methods or systems of things, the governing assumptions. Among the regimes of representation, performance and classification which are used to keep order in the media *blivit*, there exist regimes of truth. But a characteristic of all the modern media – the press, radio, cinema, publishing, television – is that, in each case, incommensurate regimes of truth coexist. The two principal regimes of truth are fact and fiction. Strenuous efforts are made, within each medium where both are found, to keep them apart. Factual and fictional truths are produced and circulated on the same channel, but by different professions, different companies or units, by different practices, in different genres with different semiotic systems and rhetorical conventions, invoking different codes of recognition and different modes of reading, for different audiences, at different times of day.

Not only do different kinds of truth result from this process, but they are maintained in an uneasy hierarchy too. A rank order is imposed in which fact is more important (has greater power to command) than fiction; the 'real' is more true than the 'imagined'. News and the domain of public affairs – the world of what E. M. Forster in *Howards End* called 'anger and telegrams' – has priority over drama and fiction.

■   ■   ■

For those who produce news, truth has the status of a professional ideology: it is what they profess. Rule 49(a) of the Constitution and Rules of the Australian Journalists' Association, for instance, sets out the *AJA Code of Ethics*: 'Respect for the truth and the public's right to information are over-riding principles for all journalists. In pursuance of these principles journalists commit themselves to ethical and professional standards', of which the first (of ten) is: 'They shall report and interpret the news with scrupulous honesty by striving to disclose all essential facts and by not suppressing relevant, available facts or distorting by wrong or improper emphasis.' The gesture of glossing 'truth' as 'facts' is, of course, characteristic of journalistic discourse, so much so that the *Style Book* of West Australian Newspapers, for instance, does not contain an entry on 'truth'. But this is what it does have to say about 'facts': 'Do not say the true, real, or actual facts. There are no untrue facts.'[4]

■   ■   ■

The domain of facts is large and varied: from the craggy heights of hard news to the lush plains of human interest, comment, current affairs, features, documentary – right up to the dangerous boundaries of 'docudrama' and even 'faction'. Or, as the BBC has put it in its own guidebook to the terrain, aimed at its own documentary producers, 'at one extreme, documentaries border on current affairs programmes; at the other, on drama'. The booklet tries to map difficult country, where, for instance, the 'material' might be documentary but the 'techniques and intention' are dramatic: such programmes 'aim more immediately at dramatic truth than at documentary truth'. Thus it asks the question: 'In its broadest form, what sort of truth ought documentaries to be concerned with?' The answers are, of course, practical, not philosophical: producers must have clear intentions; they must execute professional, responsible programmes; they must 'label' them properly both internally and in publicity; they must bear in mind differing audience interpretations and levels of engagement. These are 'the four elements which convey truth to the audience'. Philosophy is not forgotten, however: producers are 'constantly faced with questions of ethics', which boil down to what can be *simulated* and what can be *selected*. Simulation is variously glossed as 'preparation', 'fabrication', 'reconstruction', 'slightly different situations', 'go[ing] through the motions', 're-creations' and 're-enactments'. All these are 'permissible', but 'construction', 'prompting', 'invention', 'a wrong impression' and 'a fake' are not. As for selection (and editing), these are 'essential for the preservation of truth'. For instance, producers must decide whether a person featured in a programme is 'typical' or 'part of a lunatic fringe'. In the latter case, the producer must either 'present him [*sic*] clearly as such' or 'refrain from the temptation to include him at all, despite his obvious programme value'.[5]

Apart from labelling loonies or leaving them out, producers face another 'matter of great delicacy', namely how to deal with the unpredictability of 'real life' and the impossibility of conveying an 'accurate impression' of an event by simply filming it as it occurs. The two criteria for avoiding 'misunderstanding' in this area are, first, to 'give the audience a true and accurate impression of the facts' by simulating 'a true picture of a real type' of the given situation; and, second, to ensure that 'people outside television' who 'have to be present' during filming 'understand the need for the "fabrication". Otherwise dangerous seeds of doubt may be sown which could lead to a disbelief in the BBC's documentary methods.'[6]

Truth, then, turns out to be a *blivit* after all; the end product (hopefully) of a mixture of fact, fiction, fabrication and faking whose chief characteristic is that the audience – with much encouragement – continues to believe in it despite the odds. Indeed, the principal requirement for the preservation and communication of truth is that no one 'outside television' realizes that it is founded, literally, on an 'as if' premise: despite the need for 'a mass of equipment and a whole team of people', a 'great deal of [the documentary producer's] skill is devoted to presenting his [*sic*] subject matter as if the equipment and the technical processes were not there'.[7] Or, as Kurt Vonnegut himself said in another place: 'This is the secret of good storytelling: to lie, but to keep the arithmetic sound.'[8]

■ ■ ■

One way to keep the arithmetic sound is to make sure that the pictures tell the same story as the script. Even in news programmes there are unadmitted constructions which are designed to jolly along the audience by making it think that the so-called real world is like a feature film. Sound is added to recalcitrant pictures to make them tell a particular kind of truth.

These matters are rarely discussed 'outside television', but in a letter to the London *Guardian* (1 March 1985) a professional picture editor called Andrew Lewis let the cat out of the bag. He had spotted the use of sound effects in several stories put out by the commercial news organization ITN. Having a professional eye for shoddy work, he cited examples where the arithmetic had failed to add up – for instance, the use of 'hospital effects' over still photographs showing the Pope recovering in hospital, 'making the frozen Pope look like a corpse', or the addition of sound effects to 'silent video of Mount Everest, complete with car-horns going in the background'. Wondering why ITN keeps a sound-effects library at all, Lewis commented: 'It is bad enough that there is bias in what our newsreaders say. But there is no excuse for deliberately faking the relationship of sound and vision to reinforce their scripts.'

■   ■   ■

Truth is a product of struggle: struggle between technology and subject matter, certainly, but more than this. Truth is a product of war, and is itself adversarial. There is not, and never has been, an original truth, or, if there has been, the origin is that of the word 'truth' itself, where, interestingly, it is a social, discursive, adversarial sense that predominates, not an abstract, transcendental, absolute one. In Old and early Middle English, 'truth' could be glossed as steadfast allegiance, fidelity to a cause or person, faithfulness, loyalty. It was the same word as 'troth' (one's faith pledged or plighted) and as 'truce' (a singularized form of the plural of true – 'trues' – i.e. an exchange of faith to allow cessation of hostilities). In such usage, truth is not conceivable as an abstract object or a quality of an objective world that can't answer back; it is a relational or orientational term, expressing the social relations of often warring parties.

The process of abstracting and objectifying truth has, however, been going on for quite a while, though contradictorily it remains an adversarial notion. Indeed, the modern notions of truth are literally a product of war: the wars between different kinds of Christian truths that took the form of the Reformation and Counter-Reformation. One aspect of that struggle was semiotic, as it were: a war of representation, fought to decide which regime of truth, what technology of representation, whose discursive strategies would convey the most accurate impression of objective – divine – truth. The outcomes of that war have lasted right up until today.

The medieval Catholic Church was an effective mass medium. Like more recent, and more obvious, mass media, the medieval church was a complex of institutions dedicated to mass communication. It had centralized policy-making bureaucracies of great power, and included not only 'controllers' (the curia, bishops, etc.), and not only 'producers', 'presenters' and 'contributors' (professional specialists, from masons to deacons), but also 'consumers' (the laity itself), whose vast numbers dwarfed any other social community of the day, including nations, empires and language groups, just as television audiences do these days. Like television, the medieval church was riddled with internal contradictions and fierce competitive struggles, but, like television, it nevertheless spanned the known world and was designed to cut across established political, demographic and cultural boundaries. It was a force for both social cohesion and social control.

For its consumers at least, the medieval church was a peculiarly non-literate medium, conveying its truths to its audiences in audio-visual and performative form: songs, sights, stories, speech. It employed the highest, leading-edge technologies and massive capital investment to produce its hardware (cathedrals, carvings, Latin, manuscripts) and its software (liturgies, laws, rites, rituals). Its output was organized into genres, schedules and seasons, and it was dedicated to audience maximization – seeking, at least in theory, a world rating of 100 per cent. It was, like television, free at the point of consumption, but, like television, it was paid for indirectly by its consumers. Unlike television, whose truth has often been doubted, it discouraged doubts about truth with weapons that were the then equivalent of what was dropped on Hiroshima.

The Protestants, opening a competing channel, were determined to put a stop to all this. Their truth was a product of war with this mighty opponent. Among other things, the audio-visual medium of the medieval church was to be supplanted by a new medium, a new technology of truth, which was understood at the time (and still is) to be intrinsically more truthful: the medium of print. The art of printing was held to be responsible for 'the manifestation of truth, propagation of the Gospel, restoration of learning, diffusion of knowledge, and consequently the discovery and destruction of Popery'.[9] Printing shed light on the 'tedious and deep dungeons of loathsome ignorance', and the dawn of 'purer doctrine' enabled the 'liberal sciences' to disperse 'the soggy and darkened clouds of this old motheaten barbarousness'.[10]

But, like television documentary producers, the Reformation truth producers devoted a great deal of their skill to presenting their subject matter as if the equipment and the technical processes were not there. Truth was understood as a property of an objective, natural world. Its discovery was impeded by the elaborate verbal and visual arts so beloved of the opposition, but it was revealed by print. Thus the Protestants were against drama, poetry, dialogue, visual images; they were for monologic prose ('plain style'), logic, method, diagrammatic spatializations of knowledge, books. Their theory of representation held that art imitates nature: truth is attained by observation and study of nature, so that the 'truth of art' corresponds to the 'truth of nature' as a portrait should correspond to its sitter.[11] And that correspondence was understood as literal, not metaphorical: thus 'it is unknown of what form and countenance' God, Christ and the saints of antiquity were; 'wherefore, seeing that religion ought to be grounded upon truth, images, which cannot be without lies, ought not to be made'. Truth, then, was deemed to be dependent upon a one-to-one relationship between a sign and its referent, and if there was no empirical, ocular proof of the form and countenance of that referent, then any sign of it would be 'false and lying . . . the teacher of all error'.[12]

■ ■ ■

The traditional emblem of the teacher in this period was a figure of the schoolmaster holding, in either hand, the book and the rod. One of the features of those times was the escape of that figure from the confines of the classroom, from whence it tramped, militantly, across the whole social domain. A regime of truth, using the technologies of print, pedagogy and preaching, was imposed throughout the popular media of the day, promoting truth for teenagers, understanding for the 'simple people'. This popular, pedagogical truth was still adversarial, produced out of the war of words with the opposition. Naturally, the opposition was stirred up by Satan, and comprised 'cruel tyrants, sharp persecutors, and extreme enemies unto God and his infallible truth' who are 'pretending, most untruly', that reading 'God's word is an occasion of heresy and carnal liberty, and the overthrow of all good order in all well ordered commonweals'.[13]

The stakes, then, were high: threats to the soul (heresy), the private body (carnal liberty) and the public body (well-ordered commonweals), taken together, spell the end of the world. To prevent that, the Protestants were determined that their transparent, referential, natural truth should prevail. In this fight, technology and teaching were counted better allies than theology or theory. The trouble with the visual culture of the Papists was that it was a bad teacher – a teacher not only of lies but of sexy ones at that: visual images are 'trimly decked in gold, silver and stone, as well the images of men as of women, like wanton wenches ... that love paramours'; therefore, 'although it is now commonly said they be the layman's books, yet we see they teach no good lessons'. Indeed, what they teach is 'other manner of lessons, of esteeming of riches, of pride and vanity in apparel, of niceness and wantonness, and peradventure of whoredom'. So says the official *Book of Homilies*, whose message was to be 'declared and read by all parsons, vicars and curates, every Sunday and Holiday in their churches'.[14] As in those days, so in these: truth is – must be – for teenagers: 'The Bible opens with a sentence well within the writing skills of a lively fourteen-year-old'; 'any person who can't explain his work to a fourteen-year-old is a charlatan'.[15]

■ ■ ■

King James is, as is well known, the name both of a king and of the Authorized Version of the Bible (1611). What is less well known, perhaps, is that it was in his reign too that the first ever English licence to print news was issued.[16] As usual, the granting of such a licence in 1622 indicates a will to control and fix the dissemination of news as much as a willingness to encourage it. The licence covered only foreign news; the authorities permitted only Authorized Versions of domestic events. One newsworthy foreign event in that same year of 1622 was the story from Rome that Pope Gregory XV had instituted a new body of cardinals to oversee the Catholic Church's missionary work. This body was called the Congregatio de Propaganda Fide.

So entered a new word into the English language – a foreign, adversarial, oppositional word. While Protestant discourses prated constantly about 'propagation', 'diffusion', 'teaching' and 'manifestation' of the truth, and while the Reformation was noted for its missionary zeal on that truth's behalf, none of this was understood as 'propaganda'. On the contrary, propagation is a property of nature: the word applied originally to the propagation of vines, and became applied metaphorically to 'the best end of marriage' (*Oxford English Dictionary*), namely propagation of the human species. Such a term signified increase, abundance and profit too, so it was clearly not just natural but also good. Propagation of the truth, therefore, was the very opposite of what the nasty, scheming, Latin-speaking Catholics were up to. Ever since, propaganda has been understood as a term of reproach applied to secret associations for the spread of opinions and principles which are viewed by most people and governments with horror and aversion (*Oxford English Dictionary*). Even so, it wasn't too long before there were Protestant associations just like the Congregatio de Propaganda, but of course they didn't say so. What could be reproachful about 'one Body Politick and Corporate, in Deed, and in Name, by the Name of the Society for the Propagation of the Gospel in Foreign Parts', set up by Royal Charter in 1701? And what could be secret about the famous SPCK, the Society for the Propagation of Christian Knowledge?

■   ■   ■

Propaganda still has a bad name, but these days it is understood not so much as an organization as a form. Recognizing fact from fiction, or truth from propaganda, has in these days become largely a semiotic activity of learning how to recognize what regime of truth is in play at a given moment. This means, of course, that reading (and viewing and listening – the term 'reading' will be used to cover all cases) is still a highly political activity.

As is well known, war is the continuation of politics by other means. In these days – the days of Tripoli, Port Stanley, Nicaragua, Grenada, *Rainbow Warrior* – warfare is more than ever a continuation of domestic political rhetoric. Without the benefit, or embarrassment, of official institutions of propaganda, strong governments nevertheless maintain a militantly pedagogic attitude towards their citizens, and necessarily rely on the news media to popularize their truths. To supply the occasional war is to make to citizens and media alike an offer of truth that they cannot refuse.

This is what makes the politics of reading so important, since a truth is not produced by the mere act of utterance, by whatever authority, in whatever medium. A truth is produced in the act of reading. Even if there are authorial intentions, authorized versions, official manipulations or preferred readings inscribed into those utterances (all contentious claims in these days of high theory), there is still no guarantee of the semiotic, let alone the political, outcome. However, it is not enough simply to maintain that all texts are polysemic, that they don't determine what sense will be made of them, that authorial intentions are irrelevant to meanings, or even that both authors and readers are mere epiphenomena of impersonal textual and discursive processes. The politics of reading arises from the power of certain discourses, in the teeth of all this, to command assent, to mobilize social and individual action, to allow governments to burnish their truths in the glare of the television lights and then hurl them, on everyone's behalf, at the current opponent. In these days of mass democracy and mass communication, everyone is made complicit with the militant, pedagogical, adversarial, authoritative truths of the day. But these truths are also the lies of professional storytellers, and they display similar logic: 'the fatal premise of *A Connecticut Yankee* [*in King Arthur's Court*] remains a chief premise of Western civilization, and increasingly of world civilization, to wit: the sanest, most likeable persons, employing superior technology, will enforce sanity throughout the world.'[17]

The fatal premise of news is this: that it simply imitates reality or nature; it is transparent, representational and unconstructed. Therefore, so long as it avoids bias, remains impartial and sticks to plain facts in plain language, it is true.

■　　■　　■

How is it possible, then, for sane, likeable readers to recognize propaganda? Generally speaking, as far as readers are concerned, propaganda is more honest than news – it makes none of the truth-claims of news; it is the antithesis of news, precisely because its form invites a different politics of reading. Whereas news has taken the path of realistic fiction and referentiality, propaganda has taken a different path.

News is diegetic; propaganda is dialogic. News uses narrative storytelling, employing the oldest three-act plot schemes in the book: Act 1 – get a person up a tree; Act 2 – throw stones at them; Act 3 – get them down.[18] Like all storytelling forms, news is based on conflict, confrontation or struggle. The newsworthiness of an event depends on its suspense value – on how it turns out. News uses the other staples of fiction, action and character – though the characters are presented as playing themselves and the actions are presented as unconstructed (though rarely spontaneous).

Propaganda is not confined, however, to the restricted, dull, authoritarian aesthetics of news, nor to the conventions and politics of a closed, diegetic world. Whereas news and realist fiction draw readers' attention *into* the text, propaganda directs their attention *beyond* it. Where news and realist fiction resolve conflicts diegetically, within the text, propaganda provokes conflict dialogically, within the reader. News and realist fiction align the reader to the past, in which the actions portrayed have already been completed. Propaganda aligns the reader to the present and the future, towards action yet to occur. News and realist fiction position the reader as a judgemental, impartial, omniscient, voyeuristic spectator; propaganda orients the reader towards engagement or participation with an object. News, unlike realist fiction, presents itself on television as unauthored, and it uses direct address and eye-contact – these being among the semiotic devices used to set the 'real' apart from the 'fictional'. But propaganda does not seek to produce in its readers a recognition of an abstract, unauthored truth. It seeks first and foremost to produce recognition of a relationship between the addresser and the addressee, a relationship ideally of faith, allegiance, loyalty to the cause: old-style truth. News and realist fiction are enslaved to representation, to the notion that a sign stands for a referent and that's that. Propaganda is able to exploit the modernist repertoires of signification, rhetoric, pleasure and celebratory self-awareness; its skills are devoted to presenting its techniques not as 'not there', but as *here*. Both news and realist fiction seek to capture and colonize the future, filling it with the meanings and social relationships of the past. Propaganda, on the contrary, is always an ephemeral and instrumental art, seeking not to fix the future but to challenge and change it.

■   ■   ■

Even so, propaganda continues to have a bad name, perhaps because its techniques have proved so popular in publicity, advertising, pop music (video clips and promos), and in the jingles, station idents and promos, trailers, continuity and 'sniplet' shows that together stitch the *blivitous* texts of television and the press into readability. However, despite its good name for impartiality, facticity and unbiased access to unarguable truths, news still has to win readers. And in order to do this it has necessarily to compete with the pleasures, genres and distractions that surround it.

News has never been exempt from the need to con with entertainment a readership otherwise likely to be indifferent. Witness merely one of the titans of the first phase of popular newspapers, the radical 'pauper press' of the early nineteenth century. Henry Hetherington, founder of the *Poor Man's Guardian*, announced a successor to that paper in 1833. The *Twopenny Dispatch* would be 'a repository of all the gems and treasures, and fun and frolic . . . news and occurrences' of the week. 'It shall abound in Police Intelligence, in Murders, Rapes, Suicides, Burnings, Maimings, Theatricals, Races, Pugilism, and all manner of "accidents by flood and field". In short it will be stuffed with every sort of devilment that will make it sell.' This despite the fact that 'our object is not to make money, but to beat the Government'.[19] More recently, and on the other side of the political barricades, one of the archetypal press barons of the twentieth century told the same story. Lord Beaverbrook said of his *Daily Express*: 'My purpose originally was to set up a propaganda paper. . . . But in order to make the propaganda effective the paper had to be successful. No paper is any good at all for propaganda unless it has a thoroughly good financial position.'[20]

Despite Lord Beaverbrook's brave words, straightforward party propaganda did not survive the era of the press barons and the rise of mass-circulation newspapers. The paradoxical legacy of the influential barons is a newspaper business that is wholeheartedly dedicated to being 'successful' with a 'thoroughly good financial position' – a business dedicated to entertainment, not to government. Where the barons were consistent, and where they laid the framework for their modern unennobled successors, was in maximizing circulation with promotional, not directly political, campaigns.[21] The most important wars to the owners of the news media are now (as always) circulation wars. News, then, has developed within its regimes of truth a populist, promotional propaganda for itself – a politics of reading, and a pretty impoverished political platform at that, consisting ultimately in the slogan 'Read me!'

Truth is thus a product of the circulation and ratings wars for readers. One consequence of this in the modern media is that propaganda itself has become depoliticized, as it were. Instead of measuring success by winning the assent of their readers to the truth of this or that line of propaganda, the successors of Beaverbrook measure their success simply by winning readers. Their propaganda, consequently, doesn't appear to be propaganda *for* anything very much: the truth is not 'what we – the producers – say it is', but 'what you – the readers – know it is'. As a result, there is a declining proportion of news in the most-read newspapers. Even so, newspapers persist in so calling themselves, and in promoting themselves on their news – their regime of truth – despite their historic tendency towards contact with the world of the imaginary via stories about stars, celebrities and showbiz; their fetishization of bodies and faces; their mobilization of fantasies via competitions; and their devotion of upwards of 40 per cent of available space to non-editorial matter, namely advertisements. The 'quality' press is by no means exempt from these tendencies either, although its disproportionate 'influence' stems largely from the success of its regime of truth in not only reporting but also provoking anger and telegrams among its few but powerful readers. Similarly, news on television is privileged, and is used to promote the credibility of the station as a whole, while the daily news programmes are used to structure the schedules and to anchor the station to real time (and real life). News shows are thus normally exempt from the competitive mêlée of programming that surrounds them, despite their low ratings and their status as minority output (around 4 or 5 per cent of total air time – comparable with continuity). News on television and in the press, then, has survived both by becoming one of the entertainment media, and by claiming privileged exemption for itself as a genre that lends tone to the establishment.

■   ■   ■

Truth may be a product of wars (for hearts and minds, dollars and votes). But war, conversely, is now a branch of rhetoric, an entertaining pedagogical device which teaches the citizens of strong countries that they're not to be trifled with, and teaches the current opponent a lesson. The current opponent is usually personified by the leaders of small, unglamorous nations which profess an absolute or fundamental truth of their own – a nationalism rendered ludicrous by the espousal of, say, Islam (Gaddafi of Libya), communism (Ortega of Nicaragua, according to the White House), even territorial integrity (Galtieri of Argentina). What better

San Francisco Chronicle

The Largest Daily Circulation in Northern California

| Year No. 111 | ★★★★★ | SATURDAY, MAY 25, 1985 | 777-11 |

By Eric Luse

View of the Bridge — From the Bridge

Sailors dotted the flight deck of the aircraft carrier Carl Vinson yesterday as the world's largest warship passed beneath the Golden Gate Bridge on the way to its home at the Alameda Naval Air Station, completing a 7½-month, 65,000-mile voyage in the western Pacific and Indian oceans. The sailors on the Navy's newest carrier — recently adopted as 'San Francisco's Own' — received an enthusiastic welcome from families, sweethearts and friends as the ship eased into her berth at the naval air station's Pier 3. This photo, taken from the carrier's bridge, shows lights (foreground) used to direct planes. Story and another photo on Page 2.

than to wallop such dangerous, threatening truths, to prove that the inability, so far, to wallop the Russians isn't *really* impotence?

The largest single piece of equipment in the technology of truth – of the kind that was dropped on Hiroshima – displaces 95,000 tons, has a 4½-acre top and is called the *Carl Vinson*. The *Carl Vinson* is the largest aircraft carrier in the world. But its role, in these adversarial days, isn't so much propaganda as propagation: it is the flagship not for any particular truth, but for technological and bodily potency.

Kurt Vonnegut claims that 'the first story in the history of literature to have "fuck" in its title' was his own short story 'The Big Space Fuck'. It was about an American rocket ship loaded with human sperm, and sent off to Andromeda in an effort to propagate the human species: 'to make sure that human life would continue to exist somewhere in the Universe, since it certainly couldn't continue much longer on earth', what with 38-foot lampreys in Lake Erie, living on 'shit and beer cans and old automobiles and Clorox bottles'.[22]

The Big Space Fuck is, of course, a mere fiction. What actually happened was reported in the *San Francisco Chronicle* (25 May 1985). 'Sailors dotted the flight deck' = spermatozoa; 'the world's largest warship' = the world's largest penis; 'passed beneath the Golden Gate Bridge on the way to its home' = fucked. 'The sailors on the Navy's newest carrier – recently adopted as "San Francisco's Own"' = legitimate marriage; 'received an enthusiastic welcome from families, sweethearts and friends as the ship eased into her berth' = the earth moved for me too dear.

Part of the politics of reading is, of course, to persuade readers to turn the page, to the 'Story and another photo on Page 2'. The act of turning, a pregnant pause, reveals instantly the fruits of the union of warship and city: a photo of an infant held triumphantly aloft – *Ecce homo*!

The *San Francisco Chronicle* succeeds where nature has failed – simultaneous consummation and confinement. 'The huge carrier . . . made a dramatic entrance . . . after nosing through a 200-mile-thick fogbank that clung to the coast like whipped cream.' God is on hand to bless the union: 'As if on cue, the fog dissipated and the sun warmed the vast flight deck like a benediction'. The climax comes at 9.15 a.m., 'exactly on time': 'A lusty roar exploded from the 5000 homesick sailors'. Like the readers, the sailors too can instantly enjoy the sight of the fruit of their own and their wives' labours: one 'stood on the 4.5-acre flight deck and strained to see his pregnant wife'; another 'wore a big grin but could not stop his tears as he met his 2-month-old son Christopher for the first time'; indeed, there were 'about 50 new fathers who met their children for the first time yesterday along Alameda's Pier 3, where wives and families began gathering at dawn for the arrival.' If the best end of marriage is indeed the propagation of the species, then those fifty must be counted the lucky ones – or at least the ones whose photos are taken and whose words are quoted. For the rest of the lusty 5000, however, there are hints of pleasures to come: 'Some 3000 wives, sweethearts, children and other family members . . . laughed with delight as the big gray ship was pushed into her berthing spaces by

By Chris Stewart

Lieutenant Commander Sam Locklear held his 15-month-old daughter Jillian after arriving in Alameda aboard the Carl Vinson

The Carl Vinson Comes Home to the Bay

Best Part of a 65,000-Mile Voyage

By Kevin Leary

The mighty aircraft carrier arl Vinson came home to an motional and patriotic wel-ome yesterday after a 7½-1onth, 65,000-mile cruise in the estern Pacific and Indian ceans.

The huge carrier, newly adopt-d as "San Francisco's own," made a ramatic entrance into San Francis-o Bay after nosing through a 200-aile-thick fogbank that clung to the oast like whipped cream.

As if on cue, the fog dissipated nd the sun warmed the vast flight eck like a benediction as the Vin-on steamed under the Golden Gate ridge at 9.15 a.m. — exactly on me.

A lusty roar exploded from the 000 homesick sailors aboard the 5,000-ton flattop, the largest war-hip in the world and the Navy's ewest carrier,

"I'm gonna go home to Merced and be a husband to someone I've really missed for 7½ months and be a father pretty soon," said Airman Bill Lampley, 22, as he stood on the 4.5-acre flight deck and strained to see his pregnant wife waiting on the crowded pier at Alameda Naval Air Station.

"The cruise was long — really long — but there were adventures and beautiful ports most people will never get to see," said Lampley. "It's been worth it."

The voyage included one unin-terrupted stretch of 107 days at sea and rowdy liberties in the Philip-pines, Australia and Japan.

When the ship tied up at Ala-meda Naval Air Station, Airman Vincent Ayule, 22, wore a big grin but could not stop his tears as he met his 2-month-old son Christo-pher for the first time.

"Big, ain't he?" said Ayule after inspecting the red-faced, 10-pound baby. "I love him. I've been dying to see my baby. He was born on March 30 when we were in the Indian Ocean. It's tough having your first son born when you're so far away."

Ayule was one of about 50 new fathers who met their children for the first time yesterday along Ala-meda's Pier 3, where wives and fam-ilies began gathering at dawn for the arrival.

Some 3000 wives, sweethearts, children and other family members stood on the pier and waved "Wel-come Home" signs and laughed with delight as the big gray ship was pushed into her berthing spaces by straining tugboats.

"Awwwriiight!" howled a gang of sailors hanging over the port side of the ship admiring the women waiting ashore. A couple of hun-dred tossed their sailor hats like Frisbees into the waiting crowd.

Also aboard the ship yesterday were 1200 civilian relatives — all male — whom the Navy invited aboard in Pearl Harbor for a free six-day trip aboard the Vinson for the last 2398-mile leg of the voyage home.

"We had a wonderful time," said Carlton Da Vega, 54, of Santa Rosa, who joined his 21-year-old son, Flight Crewman Eric Da Vega, on the trip from Hawaii to San Francis-co.

"Everything was great," said the senior Da Vega, obviously proud of his sailor son. "Then last Sunday they put on a terrific live fire exer-cise that you wouldn't believe. Bombing and strafing. It was very impressive. The firepower of this ship is awesome."

The Vinson will be in port for three months for refitting. She is expected to take another extended cruise next fall.

By Howard Erker/The Tribune

Home at last!

Framed by a colorful arch of balloons, the USS Carl Vinson, the nation's largest and newest nuclear carrier, glided into its home port yesterday at Alameda Naval Air Station after a 7½-month tour of duty. Part of its crew of 5,000, including 99 who became fathers while at sea, lined the flight decks for the reunion with relatives. More photos, Page A-8.

straining tugboats. "Awwwriiight!" howled a gang of sailors . . . admiring the women waiting ashore.' But for them all there is a significance beyond pleasure. Their potency signifies that of the 'big gray ship': 'A couple of hundred tossed their sailor hats like Frisbees into the waiting crowd.' And the potency of the carrier matches theirs: ' ". . . last Sunday they put on a terrific live fire exercise that you wouldn't believe. Bombing and strafing. It was very impressive. The firepower of this ship is awesome." '

■   ■   ■

The firepower of this story arises from its status as truth. Truth is easy to recognize. The event happened 'yesterday', and makes the front page in several local newspapers. In this sixteen-paragraph story there are twenty-four numerical facts, ten place-names, seven named people and six direct-speech quotations. But there are attributes to these facts too – just as true, but more entertaining. There are thirty-odd adjectives, applying mostly

Home are the sailors...

Mrs. Joette Sperlich, above left, made a last-minute makeup check before welcoming her husband, Navy Lt. Cmdr. James Sperlich, among those returning to home port in Alameda aboard the nuclear aircraft carrier USS Carl Vinson. Greeting one another during the arrival yesterday, above right, are Lt. Cmdr. Tony Racette and his wife, Donna, holding baby Ashley. Right in the middle of it all is daughter Tara.

to the *Carl Vinson* (mighty, huge, vast, largest, newest, big, gray, dramatic, exactly, straining) or to the sailors and their families (lusty, homesick, pregnant, crowded, rowdy, big, red-faced, new, male, civilian). And the similes – 'like whipped cream', 'like a benediction', 'like Frisbees' – are just the sort of 'visual' images that together with the photographs themselves are already clichéd in pop videos: the familiar correspondences between technology and sex, the divine and the domestic, don't have to be stated. They can be seen to be true. But they are more important than the facts in producing an agreed meaning for the event. The Oakland *Tribune* (25 May 1985) also reported it, with different facts (ninety-nine new fathers, not fifty, and different individuals), but with the very same significance.

Neither story mentions an actual or potential adversary against whom the 'awesome firepower' might be directed, and neither says anything about nuclear weapons. The purpose of the 7½-month, 65,000-mile 'cruise' is restricted to a passing reference in the *San Francisco Chronicle* to 'one uninterrupted stretch of 107 days at sea and rowdy liberties in the Philippines, Australia and Japan'. This was not the first visit of the *Carl Vinson* to Australia. In July 1983 there had been another 'rowdy liberty' in Fremantle, and the Australian press had understood it in just the same way as the Californian press understood the *Carl Vinson*'s 1985 return. The Melbourne *Age* (4 July 1983) reported that the John Curtin High School in Fremantle had instituted eight daily truancy checks, one every forty minutes, to stop 'scores of girls' being 'away for days on end with newly acquired American boyfriends, many of them met through the "Dial a Sailor Service" organized by the US Navy and given wide publicity in the Perth media'. However, the same story does contain a reminder of other, popular, truths: 9000 people, in the 'biggest anti-nuclear demonstration ever seen' in Western Australia, 'linked arms . . . to form a human chain more than two kilometres long' to protest against the presence of 'nuclear armed American vessels in their port, including the . . . Carl Vinson, the newest, most sophisticated warship in the US Navy'.

Even so, 9000 protesters did not get the last word. That went to Lieutenant-Commander John Whittaker, senior Australian recruiting officer in Western Australia, who warned the 5000 US sailors to 'be prepared for these clowns', since 'one of the problems of democracy is that every idiot will have his say'. The Brisbane *Sun* (2 July 1983) also reported his speech, adding: ' "You'll get what you want ashore in Perth, whatever that may be," Cdr Whittaker assured the cheering crew of the USS Carl Vinson. . . . "the birds will be interested. Everyone in Perth will be interested and friendly except one group" ' (the anti-nuclear protesters), but ' "You'll meet a bird and all you'll be interested in will be indoor sports . . ." '

■   ■   ■

One of the problems of democracy is that it is all too easy for some idiots to have their say. For others it is much more difficult. It is the teachers, not the taught, who do most of the talking in the pedagogic modern media; 9000 'people' are no match for a Lieutenant-Commander. The consequence of this arithmetic is that when a producer or reporter tries, as Ken Loach did in his British series *Questions of Leadership* (1983), made for Channel Four Television, to show people who have 'rarely, if ever, been seen on national television, putting views that are never acknowledged',[23] then such stories are accused of bias, propaganda, half-truth – and they are banned. Who were the dangerous 'people' in Loach's films? They were trade-unionists, not the leaders but the led. And what, asks Loach, caused the IBA to shelve the films? 'I believe it was because we touched on the most sensitive political nerve. . . . Working people explain in the films how their leaders have confused, demoralized, and sabotaged the struggle to prevent closures and defend living standards. . . . Union leaders have failed to organize the strength of the labour movement. They have, in effect, kept the Tories in power.' Thus a series that 'enabled trade unionists to recount incidents and experiences that provoked questions about the political directions of their unions'[24] also provoked a politics of reading among the administrators, who read the 'message' on behalf of an untrustworthy audience, pronounced it 'unbalanced', and scuppered the series.

Of course, Loach's series wasn't exactly banned. Its effective censorship was achieved, 'not by an outright ban but by delay and inaction, by passing the item from one desk to another, so that the programme gradually loses its topicality and relevance'.[25] The most notorious example of a victim of this process is Peter Watkins's film *The War Game*, made as a documentary for the BBC in 1965. Despite the opinion of senior BBC executives – Grace Wyndam Goldie (Head of Television Talks) and Huw Wheldon – at the time that 'so long as there is no security risk and the facts are authentic, the people should be trusted with the truth',[26] they were not so trusted by the BBC until 4,400,000 of them watched it twenty years later, in August 1985 (the fortieth anniversary of Hiroshima) on the minority channel BBC2.[27]

One that got away was the Australian Broadcasting Corporation's film report called *Black Death*, dealing with the deaths of Aborigines in police or prison custody in Western Australia, and screened in the ABC's *Four Corners* slot in September 1985. According to the Perth *West Australian* (25 September 1985), the programme was hailed by the Aboriginal Legal Service, who 'said it was an accurate reflection of concerns felt by Aborigines over prison deaths'. However, the police and prison officers' unions, and their legal representatives, said it was nothing but lies; their barrister 'said the programme was the most disgraceful example of biased, unfair and untrue reporting that he had ever seen', while the secretary of the Western Australian police union 'said there were blatant untruths throughout the programme'. As a result, the police banned ABC TV reporters from their briefings on all other matters in Western Australia, and refused their crews admittance to police premises – a bizarre procedure that the crews duly filmed for the ABC's *National* news programme. There were moves to have the reporter responsible for *Black Death*, David Marr, extradited from New South Wales to Western Australia to face charges of criminal libel, and various civil cases were initiated. Both the police and prison officers' unions lodged complaints with the Australian Journalists' Association, claiming that Marr had breached the first standard of the AJA Code of Ethics. This move had the curious effect of allowing that part of the code to be quoted in full on the front page of the *West Australian*, giving readers a rare glimpse of that paper's own regime of truth from the professionals' point of view.

■ ■ ■

Thus do the upholders of public truths defend themselves. Their wrath was directed at a television corporation and a reporter – certainly both well able to defend themselves in turn – but the occasion of that wrath, the 'biased, unfair, untrue', was simply another kind of truth; not natural, unauthored, eternal or 'representative', but the truth of some of those people who have rarely, if ever, been seen on national television, putting views that are never acknowledged. The strong and no doubt honestly held idea that such truths are not only propagandist and biased, but actually untrue, is itself a product of the prevailing regime of truth in the popular media. While the 'meaning' of the largest nuclear weapon in the world is 'naturally' to do with propagation, and goes unchallenged, the truths of such groups as nuclear disarmers, trade-unionists and workers, Aborigines and even 'the people', are inadmissible; capable of being reported, if at all, only as the wild ravings of clowns and idiots on the lunatic fringe. And such groups rarely have the organized power or institutional clout to hit back at the media, whereas politicians, police and other representatives of the world of anger and telegrams do.

Thus the forces of truth are unequally balanced. As a result, journalists have arrived at a set of restrictive, defensive rules about 'balance' which are designed primarily to keep politicians off their backs. Commenting on this situation, the then Political Editor of the London *Sunday Times*, Hugo Young, argued that in these days of political and audio-visual fragmentation, with multiple political parties and more screen outlets, the preservation of balance 'won't make for stimulating television. Nor do such defensive rules of journalism have much connection with arriving at truth.' However, Young concluded that these rules of balance are not a result of journalistic criteria at all, but are based on politicians' interference with the media, an interference that is 'rooted in terror. They are frightened of what they conceive to be television's power, and of what effect unorthodox opinion on the screen (about nuclear disarmament, for example) might have on the untutored populace.'[28]

In the examples cited by Young, it becomes clear that it isn't even the opinions of the 'untutored populace' as such that so scare their political teachers, but rather the 'unorthodox opinions' of 'critical' individuals within their own ranks. Thus, said Young, the producer of the BBC's flagship current affairs programme, *Panorama*, was 'called a traitor and the BBC chairman almost torn limb from limb' after part of one *Panorama* programme was given over to MPs critical of the Falklands War. 'The pressure', wrote Young, 'was effective. Very little was televised from the critics after that. It was also shocking. It showed . . . how unable they [politicians] are to accept a deviation from the orthodoxies they define.'[29]

■   ■   ■

Orthodoxy in the realm of public affairs doesn't even extend to the limits of the two major parties, let alone beyond them to the opinions of the 'untutored populace' at large. Meanwhile, party and national leaderships themselves assiduously cultivate their own particular, partial home-truths, exploiting the media, especially television, to such an extent that there surely can be no such thing as an 'untutored' populace any more, if there ever was. It is only untutored in very specific areas of the political curriculum: areas of unorthodox truth generated from unofficial sources, especially from among sections of the populace itself. But, in these days of representative democracies and balanced television, such areas appear as unrepresentative, therefore undemocratic, therefore propaganda. Thus representative (and representational) truth is a weapon in the constant war against 'unorthodox' (but popular) opinions; it is a pedagogy for an over-tutored populace who cannot be trusted with any other kind of truth because they never have been.

It is time – in these days of *blivitous*, simulated, selected, constructed, warlike, Protestant, pedagogic, representational, diegetic, representative, entertaining, numerical, impartial, godlike and terrified truths – it is time, as Hugo Young put it, 'to be unbalanced'. It is time to promote the 'disgraceful' ('displeasing to God') example of 'biased, unfair, untrue' reporting of the voices and faces of the idiots and clowns on the lunatic fringe. Otherwise, as Kurt Vonnegut feared, sanity may well be enforced throughout the world, by the *Carl Vinson*, but there may be no world left to applaud the result. It is time, in short, for propaganda to be taken seriously – which entails trusting the untutored populace to engage for itself in the politics of reading. In days such as these, the truth media should admit that their notion of truth and their means of arriving at it are incommensurable; they should admit the secret of the *blivit* and follow Vonnegut's lying but honest storytellers, whose premise is not 'this is God's truth', but merely the much less fatal 'Keep your hat on. We may wind up miles from here.'[30]

Murdoch University, Perth, Western Australia.

Notes

1 Kurt Vonnegut, *Palm Sunday: An Autobiographical Collage* (London: Cape, 1981), p. 14.
2 Ibid., p. 223.
3 Ibid., p. 13.
4 *WAN Style Book* (Perth: West Australian Newspapers, 1973), p. 36.
5 BBC Television Service, *Principles and Practice in Documentary Programmes* (London: BBC, 1972), 'drawn up' by Richard Cawston (Head of Documentary Programmes), Stephen Hearst (Head of Arts Features), Robert Reid (Head of Science Features), Anthony de Lotbinière (Producer, Documentary Programmes), Antony Jay (writer, former Head of Talks Features and former Editor of *Tonight*), Roger Cary (Secretariat), at the request of Huw Wheldon (Managing Director, BBC Television), pp. 14, 6, 15, 20–2.
6 Ibid., pp. 20–1.
7 Ibid., p. 7.
8 Vonnegut, op. cit., p. 165.
9 Silvester Jourdan, *A Plaine Description of the Barmudas, now called Sommer Ilands* (1613), quoted in Robert Foster Jones, *The Triumph of the English Language* (Stanford, Cal.: Stanford University Press, 1953), pp. 32–4 n. (spelling updated).
10 Walter Haddon, *Against Ierome Osorious* (1581), quoted in Jones, op. cit., pp. 32–4 n. (spelling updated).

11 Peter Ramus, *Training in Dialectic* (1543), quoted in Walter J. Ong, *Ramus: Method, and the Decay of Dialogue: From the Art of Discourse to the Art of Reason* (Cambridge, Mass.: Harvard University Press, 1958), pp. 175–80 (trans. from the Latin by Walter J. Ong).

12 *The Book of Homilies: Certain Sermons Appointed by the Queen's Majesty to be declared and read by all Parsons, Vicars and Curates, every Sunday and Holiday in their Churches; and by Her Grace's advice perused and overseen for the better understanding of the simple people* (1574; repr. Cambridge: Cambridge University Press, 1850), pp. 218–19.

13 Ibid., title and p. 369.

14 Ibid., pp. 177, 265 and title.

15 Vonnegut, op. cit., pp. 85, 157.

16 Stanley Harrison, *Poor Men's Guardians* (London: Lawrence & Wishart, 1974), p. 10.

17 Vonnegut, op. cit., p. 167.

18 Frances Taylor Patterson, *Cinema Craftsmanship: A Book for Photoplaywrights* (New York: Harcourt, Brace & Howe, 1920), p. 8.

19 Quoted in Harrison, op. cit., p. 98.

20 Royal Commission on the Press, *Minutes of Evidence: Twenty-Sixth Day*, Cmnd 7416 (London: HMSO, 1948), para. 8660; quoted in Graham Murdock and Peter Golding, 'The structure, ownership and control of the press 1914–76', in George Boyce, James Curran and Pauline Wingate (eds), *Newspaper History: From the Seventeenth Century to the Present Day* (London: Constable, 1978; Beverly Hills, Cal.: Sage, 1978), p. 142.

21 James Curran and Jean Seaton, *Power without Responsibility: The Press and Broadcasting in Britain*, 2nd edn (London: Methuen, 1985), ch. 5.

22 Vonnegut, op. cit., pp. 214–15.

23 Ken Loach, 'Broadcasters who uphold the established order through the charade of impartiality', *The Guardian*, 31 October 1985.

24 Ibid.

25 Ibid.

26 Quoted in Michael Tracey, 'Censored: the *War Game* story', in Crispin Aubrey (ed.), *Nukespeak: The Media and the Bomb* (London: Comedia, 1982), pp. 38–54.

27 *The Listener*, 15 August 1985, 'National Top Tens'.

28 Hugo Young, 'Time to be unbalanced' *Sunday Times*, 1 August 1982.

29 Ibid.

30 Vonnegut, op. cit., p. 166.

The picture on p. 49 is (c) *San Francisco Chronicle* 1985 and is reproduced by permission of that newspaper.

The pictures on p. 53 are reproduced by permission of *The Tribune*, Oakland, California.

JOHN FROW

ACCOUNTING FOR TASTES: SOME PROBLEMS IN BOURDIEU'S SOCIOLOGY OF CULTURE

> Taste classifies, and it classifies the classifier. Social subjects, classified by their classifications, distinguish themselves by the distinctions they make, between the beautiful and the ugly, the distinguished and the vulgar, in which their position in the objective classifications is expressed or betrayed.[1]

Pierre Bourdieu's *Distinction: A Social Critique of the Judgement of Taste* completes what is perhaps the strongest case we have about the social functions of cultural artefacts; but it is a case that is deeply flawed. In this article I try to isolate some of the theoretical presuppositions and implications of its central concepts, and to clarify their political limitations.

The subtitle of Bourdieu's first book in the area of cultural practice, *Un Art moyen: essai sur les usages sociaux de la photographie*, indicates how his interest is focused: he and his collaborators are concerned not with an aesthetics of photography (although, paradoxically, something like this emerges in the book) but with the social uses it is put to; specifically, they analyse the normative structures of aesthetic legitimacy in relation to which photographic practices are structured, and the way this relation then produces different conceptions of what photography is or should be – different sets of aesthetic standards – among different classes of practitioners. In a subsequent book, *L'Amour de l'art: les musées d'art européens et leur public*, Bourdieu and Darbel reject the assumption that there is a universal and undifferentiated public of the state-run art galleries – that 'everyone' goes – in order to conduct a statistical analysis of who precisely does visit them. What they found was that their public is differentiated along class lines or, more precisely (the difference is important), in terms of levels of education and in terms of cultural aspiration rather than achieved position. The statistics are stark: most working-class people don't go to art galleries, especially when difficult modern art is being exhibited; when they do go they stay for less time than middle-class and upper-class people (an average stay of 22, 35 and 47 minutes respectively); and the *musée d'art* reminds them of a church rather than of a library or a store. Experiencing a mixture of hostility and deference, working-class people choose to reject

59

the alienating institutions of legitimate culture, and this means that access to cultural goods 'is the privilege of the cultivated class; but this privilege has all the trappings of legitimacy. In effect, the only ones excluded are those who exclude themselves.'[2]

In *Distinction*, which draws in part on the earlier work, Bourdieu has produced a book with the 'perhaps immoderate ambition of giving a scientific answer to the old questions of Kant's critique of judgement, by seeking in the structure of the social classes the basis of the systems of classification which structure perception of the social world and designate the objects of aesthetic enjoyment' (p. xiv). Using extensive survey material administered over a number of years, Bourdieu sets aesthetic practice in relation to a range of other practices of 'taste', in order to reconstruct the systematic unity of class 'lifestyles', which in turn are generated by that system of 'durable dispositions' he calls the *habitus*. Thus, in addition to being asked about their preferences in painting, music and photographic themes, the interview subjects were questioned about choices in interior decoration, clothing, food and politics; and additional evidence is adduced concerning the social differentiation of the body and of language use.[3] In the course of this investigation the book amasses a wealth of material about the distribution of tastes within the system of French culture.

The point of this is not to establish the truism that different classes adopt different lifestyles, but to explore the process by which differences in cultural preference become socially functional. It is a question not of differences in themselves but of the ability of the dominant class to impose the value given to these differences: to impose a recognition of the distinction between 'good' taste and 'vulgar' taste, between legitimate and illegitimate styles. Aesthetic judgements, then, do not obey an autonomous aesthetic logic; they transpose distinctions of class into distinctions of taste, and thereby strengthen the boundaries between classes. But they also assert the right of a ruling class to legitimate domination over other classes. Bourdieu argues this through an economic metaphor that he takes from Bernstein: competence in cultural codes constitutes a 'cultural capital' which is unequally distributed among social classes (although it has the appearance of an innate talent, a 'natural gift'). When invested in the exercise of taste, cultural capital yields both 'a profit in distinction, proportionate to the rarity of the means required to appropriate [cultural products], and a profit in legitimacy, the profit par excellence, which consists in the fact of feeling justified in being (what one is), being what it is right to be' (p. 228).

Cultural capital is generated in the schooling system, and Bourdieu here draws on his extensive work in the sociology of education. Very briefly, the relevant part of his argument is that cultural practices and preferences are linked in a two-step process to educational level and social origin, where the latter both reinforces and is discontinuous with the former. The function of the schooling system is to naturalize the streamings imposed by the social system, and in particular to valorize the systemic indeterminacy, the moments of exception, which disprove the rule of streaming. The statistical reproduction of the class structure thereby becomes perceived as a question of individual merit. What the schooling system works to reproduce, therefore, is not 'culture' in the sense of a cultural capital that belongs to the 'whole of society', but rather the structure of distribution of this cultural capital (and in the long run the social structure itself).[4] This process is complicated, however, by the ideological opposition played out within the ruling class between two modes of acquisition of culture: a scholastic mode, correlated with educational capital (and stigmatized for its visibility, its laboriousness); and a charismatic mode, correlated with inherited cultural capital.

At times Bourdieu takes the charismatic mode as characterizing all 'high' cultural practices; at other times he restricts it to the practices of the *dominant* fraction of the ruling class – the fraction that possesses economic capital (this is the first of a number of ambiguities concerning the putative unity of the ruling class). To the charismatic mode corresponds a mythology of the 'pure' gaze, of a naturally given taste: a mythology predicated on the forgetting of the process of acquiring cultural competence. This mythology

> owes its plausibility and its efficacy to the fact that, like all the ideological strategies generated in the everyday class struggle, it *naturalizes* real differences, converting differences in the mode of acquisition of culture into differences of nature; it only recognizes as legitimate the relation to culture (or language) which least bears the visible marks of its genesis, which has nothing 'academic', 'scholastic', 'bookish', 'affected' or 'studied' about it, but manifests by its ease and naturalness that true culture is nature – a new mystery of immaculate conception. (p. 68)

By contrast, the specificity of the practices of the *dominated* fraction of the ruling class (the intelligentsia, which possesses only cultural capital) is never adequately defined. For Bourdieu it would presumably consist above all in the foregrounding and estrangement of formal structures – that is, in a certain willed clumsiness, an asceticism which renounces 'ease' and which valorizes symbolic over material appropriations of works of art. In both cases, however, legitimate culture is defined by its opposition to the 'vulgar' or 'common' – aesthetic epithets which carry a displaced class content.

Thus the principle of the pleasure involved in ('high') cultural practice 'lies, in the last analysis, in the denied experience of a social relationship of membership and exclusion' (p. 400). What Bourdieu now calls 'the aesthetic disposition', meaning by this the practices and preferences of the ruling class alone, is dependent upon a distance from need, a 'generalized capacity to neutralize ordinary urgencies and to bracket off practical ends' (p. 54), which links together the owners of economic and cultural capital (and which effectively blurs the difference between the two forms of capital). From here the argument proceeds in three stages. First, the aesthetic disposition is defined as conforming to the principles of a Kantian aesthetic which severs the work of art from worldly ends and practical functions. Second, this aesthetic is then equated with an essential class experience: the aesthetic disposition 'presupposes the distance from the world . . . which is the basis of the bourgeois experience of the world' (p. 54). Finally, this correlation is then raised to a more general level: 'position in the classification struggle depends on position in the class structure' (p. 484); the one can be read off from the other.[5]

Two forms of essentialism operate in this argument. The first involves positing a single class 'experience' common to the sociologically quite distinct groups Bourdieu includes in the dominant class. The second posits a single aesthetic logic which corresponds to this experience. Together they suggest that there is an intrinsic logic of cultural practices which matches the intrinsic logic of a unitary ruling-class structure. And one of the effects of this is a binary construction of the concepts of a 'high' and a 'popular' aesthetic understood as something like class languages, fixed and ahistorical class dispositions with a necessary categorial structure.

Whereas the dominant aesthetic is associated with an autotelic formalism, a refusal of practical or ethical function, a refusal of the facile and the vulgar, and with intertextual rather than mimetic modes of reference, the 'popular' aesthetic is defined as having a primarily ethical basis and as subordinating artistic practice to socially regulated functions (for example, working-class people use photography above all for the ritual celebration of family unity).[6] In a rejection of the Kantian prescriptions,

> everything takes place as if the 'popular aesthetic' were based on the affirmation of continuity between art and life, which implies the subordination of form to function, or, one might say, on a refusal of the refusal which is the starting point of the high aesthetic, i.e. the clear-cut separation of ordinary dispositions from the specifically aesthetic disposition. (p. 32)

Thus working-class audiences are (the sense is: inherently) hostile to formal experimentation, and 'their reluctance or refusal springs not just from lack of familiarity but from a deep-rooted demand for participation, which formal experiment systematically disappoints' (pp. 32–3). It is worth noting that the *reasons* for this hostility are not given by Bourdieu's elaborate apparatus of sociological enquiry: he extrapolates them on the basis of a particular construction of working-class experience and of working people's 'deep-rooted demands'. Moreover, the aesthetic he proposes as characteristic of the working class is a conservative realist aesthetic. It could as well be defined in negative terms: as a refusal to consider the intertextual dimension of formal structures, and the social force of this intertextuality; as a lack of critical awareness of the codes through which reality effects are constructed. And, despite his denunciations of populism, Bourdieu sets up a very conventional opposition – as though of the authentic to the inauthentic – of popular culture to a 'mass market' culture (above all, television) in which 'dispossession of the very intention of determining one's own ends is combined with a more insidious form of recognition of dispossession' (p. 386). The opposition confirms the essentialism by which the image of 'the people' is constructed.

If (like the concepts of elaborated and restricted code for Bernstein) the 'high' and the 'popular' aesthetics work primarily as class languages, they are also conceived in terms of differing orientations to the process of signification. This is expressed as a set towards either the 'form' or the 'content' of the message; and on to this primary opposition is grafted a loaded secondary opposition between the categories 'cold' and 'distant' on the one hand, and 'warm' and 'participatory' on the other. Thus the 'conspicuous formality' of the ruling-class ethos implies

> a sort of censorship of the expressive content which explodes in the expressiveness of popular language, and by the same token, a distancing, inherent in the calculated coldness of all formal exploration, a refusal to communicate concealed at the heart of the communication itself, both in an art which takes back and refuses what it seems to deliver and in bourgeois politeness, whose impeccable formalism is a permanent warning against the temptation of familiarity. (p. 34)

Aesthetic distance – which Bourdieu equates with 'distance' from economic necessity – works 'by displacing the interest from the "content", characters, plot, etc., to the form, to the specifically artistic effects which are only appreciated relationally, through a comparison with other works which is incompatible with immersion in the singularity of the work immediately given' (p. 34). A double displacement, then: from the text as it is 'immediately given', and from the immediacy of life on to which the text would otherwise transparently open – since formal complexity 'throws the thing itself into the background and precludes direct communion with the beauty of the world' (p. 43).

The phrasing perhaps indicates that we should take a little readerly distance at this point: that Bourdieu, aware of the extent to which aesthetic arguments are always already inscribed in class positions, is here ironically adopting the language of the popular aesthetic itself. This is doubtless also true of a later sentence arguing that 'often the only escape from ambivalence or indeterminacy towards language is to fall back on what we *can* appreciate, the body rather than words, substance rather than form, an honest face rather than a smooth tongue' (p. 465). And yet whatever irony there is here doesn't modify the congruence of these sentences with Bourdieu's general line of argument. Having written with such force (above all in *Outline of a Theory of Practice*) against forms of essentialism and substantialism in social theory, Bourdieu falls effortlessly into both when it comes to the aesthetic. It should hardly be necessary to repeat the argument against the form/content dichotomy as Bourdieu employs it, but briefly it is this: that it places content outside the domain of the formal, and that it places the formal outside the domain of content. Coupled in this way, the categories are complicit in a naïve mimeticism rather than being capable of accounting for it.

Part of the problem is that Bourdieu is not interested in giving a detached 'account' of aesthetic codes. Despite the elaborate sociological apparatus and despite the commitment to a rigorously scientific relativism, his text is at this point almost explicitly interventionist, working to discount 'aesthetic' experience (understood as primarily an experience of form) and to valorize the directness of the working-class relation to the world. But the implicit supposition that one class stands in a more 'natural', less mediated relation to experience than do other classes is a romantic obfuscation. Bourdieu comes close to taking popular cultural forms as 'authentic' manifestations of working-class life, fully expressive of an autonomous class ethos – and this is made all the easier by the exclusion of 'mass' cultural forms from the definition of the popular. It is as though unified systems of class values were insulated from each other in completely distinct domains.

What gets overlooked here is the question of the relationality of cultural forms. Aesthetic choices are not made in a vacuum: they are made in negative relation to the other *kinds* of objects which could have been chosen, and this involves both the historical sequence to which an object belongs and its position within a synchronic system. To assert a preference (to take a book off the shelf, to tune into a radio station, to look at one picture rather than another) means using an unequally distributed cultural competence to evaluate a text in relation to these interlocking systems of relations. Now, Bourdieu's survey material, and the charts he constructs on the basis of it, do in fact set up rough models of these formations of value (formations which are, as I shall argue, only partly superimposable on social classes). Thus the survey questions on popular singers and on 'classical' music are made to yield various kinds of systemic ranking on a scale of legitimacy and difficulty: across the field, a ranking going from Georges Guétary, Petula Clark, Georges Brassens and Léo Ferré, to 'The Blue Danube', 'The Sabre Dance', *The Well-Tempered Clavier* and the 'Concerto for Left Hand'; and within classical music a class-correlated ranking going from *The Well-Tempered Clavier* to the *Rhapsody in Blue* to 'The Blue Danube' (pp. 19–20). But, while recognizing that choices made by the *dominant* class are fully relational, Bourdieu is much more ambivalent about how choices are made within the 'popular' aesthetic. This ambivalence centres on the question of the distribution of cultural competences.

A similar argument is made in both *L'Amour de l'art* and *Distinction*. It supposes that 'a work of art has meaning and interest only for someone who possesses the cultural competence, that is, the code, into which it is encoded'. This competence is crucial for the construction of textual significance: the beholder or listener or reader 'cannot move from the "primary stratum of the meaning we can grasp on the basis of our ordinary experience" to the "stratum of secondary meanings", i.e. the "level of the meaning of what is signified", unless he possesses the concepts which go beyond the sensible properties and which identify the specifically stylistic properties of the work' (pp. 2–3; the phrases quoted are from Panofsky). But one of the effects of the unequal distribution of competences by the schooling system is that members of the dominated classes do tend not to have mastery over the 'specifically aesthetic' codes, and tend to substitute for them a set of borrowed non-aesthetic categories: 'When faced with legitimate works of art, people most lacking the specific competence apply to them the perceptual schemes of their own ethos, the very ones which structure their everyday perception of everyday existence' (p. 44). Ethical and practical judgements are brought to bear on works of art understood as the more or less realistic and unmediated expression of a content.

The earlier form of the argument, in *L'Amour de l'art*, opposes this way of treating the work of art, 'as a simple means of communication transmitting a transcendent meaning [*signification*]', to a properly aesthetic reception, which, rather than detaching the text from any context, relates it to the context of other works of art.[7] The 'popular' aesthetic would thus be not a *different* set of aesthetic codes, but a way of using codes of everyday judgement rather than codes of aesthetic judgement in the appropriation of works of art. And the earlier book suggests that this entails important disadvantages for those deprived of aesthetic competence:

> An understanding of the 'expressive' and, if I may use the word, 'physiognomic' qualities of the work is an inferior form of the aesthetic experience because, unable to be sustained, controlled, and corrected by a properly iconological knowledge, it uses a key [*chiffre*] which is neither adequate nor specific.[8]

The concept of 'deprivation' is itself unsatisfactory because it accepts as given the norms of high culture. Cultural disadvantage is, in fact, operative only *on the ground of high culture*. Bourdieu assumes that the legitimacy of this ground is still imposed on the dominated classes; but it may well be the case, particularly since the massive growth of a television culture in which working-class people tend to be fully competent, that it has become largely irrelevant. (Bourdieu never seeks to *establish* the case for the legitimacy of high culture; he simply assumes it – and he pays little attention to television.) On the other hand, however, the theory of cultural disadvantage does work better, in the framework set by Bourdieu's own account of cultural exclusion and distinction, than his later valorization of the popular aesthetic for its espousal of 'content' and of 'human' values. Again, the value of 'human content' is never explicitly argued for; it is presented only by a double negation, as when, noting that respondents with high levels of cultural capital reject images of a first communion, a sunset or a landscape as subjects likely to produce a 'beautiful' photograph, Bourdieu suggests that this rejection is motivated by the fact that the images are, 'in Ortega y Gasset's terms, "naïvely human" ' (p. 35). Differing class judgements are described, that is to say, in terms of a differential relation to the photographic 'content', and this content is assumed to have a fixed meaning ('sunset' = 'human'). But of course this is not the case: meanings are not given in texts but are constructed in the relations between texts. The value of the image of a sunset cannot be read off from a photograph, but involves rather the *position* of this image within the system of similar images – a system which possesses a certain statistical frequency and density, a certain sociocultural value. Having a specific competence in this case would mean being able to make an educated guess (literally) about the extent to which the image is culturally saturated and so informationally redundant, a guess about its place within a complex intertextual system.

In the same way, Bourdieu draws too simplistic a conclusion from the strategies of negation which characterize self-conscious artistic production. Thus he writes:

> it is scarcely necessary to establish that the work of art is the objectification of a relationship of distinction and that it is thereby explicitly predisposed to bear such a relationship in the most varied contexts. As soon as art becomes self-conscious, in the work of Alberti, for example, as Gombrich demonstrates, it is defined by a negation, a refusal, a renunciation, which is the very basis of the refinement in which a distance is marked from the simple pleasure of the senses and the superficial seductions of gold and ornaments that ensnare the vulgar taste of the Philistines. (p. 227)

The implication is that this refusal is no more than the translation into the medium of painting of a gesture of snobbery. But this refusal is surely mediated by the function and value of 'sensual' painterly codes in the aesthetic domain, their overdetermination not as 'popular' codes (in the full and naturalizing sense Bourdieu gives the word – 'the simple pleasure of the senses') but as codes appropriated and automatized by an art market. Even were Bourdieu correct, however, in assigning a function of exclusion and distinction to artistic practices like those codified by Alberti, his argument would still be wrong because it would still be radically reductive. To write that the 'legitimate culture of class societies' is 'a product of domination predisposed to express or legitimate domination' (p. 228) is to assign a single and exclusive function to cultural practice, and to assume that the work of the text is exhausted in this function. Bourdieu is thereby quite unable to account for the possibility that 'legitimate' works of art might nevertheless be capable of exercising a critical function over and above their other functions.

It is the rigidity with which Bourdieu opposes two formally and functionally autonomous aesthetic universes that constitutes the problem. The immediate correlation of these aesthetic universes with social classes means that cultural forms are understood as non-contradictory expressive unities rather than as sites of political tension. Thus it becomes impossible to read, for example, a painting by Goya in terms of contradictions between its functions of cognition and exclusion, or indeed of its changing and potentially contradictory relation to the art market-place; and, conversely, the kind of political analysis that informs the work of, say, Stedman Jones on the music hall, or Willis on working-class counter-school culture, or Sennett and Cobb on the ethos of self-sacrifice in the American working class[9] – work which stresses the ideological and political ambiguity of popular cultural forms – is equally impossible in this account. I stress these *political* deficiencies because much of the recent reception of Bourdieu in English has accepted his account of the popular aesthetic in a quite uncritical manner.[10]

There is, however, a further theoretical problem in Bourdieu's work on culture which raises equally serious questions about the work's political consequences. This is the problem of how Bourdieu theorizes the relation between cultural capital and economic capital – or, to put it differently, the relation between the intelligentsia and the dominant class. Bourdieu defines class in terms of three variables: the volume of capital possessed; the composition of this capital (that is, the relation between economic and cultural capitals); and the change in volume and composition over time (the relation between past and potential trajectories). Within the dominant class 'the structure of the distribution of economic capital is symmetrical and opposite to that of cultural capital' (p. 120), and this means both that the two forms of capital are mutually exclusive, and that – in so far as possession of either is a sufficient criterion for classification in the dominant class – they are in some way mutually convertible. Their structural difference is subordinated to their potential equivalence. But of course this argument is incomplete: in the first place because the conversion of capitals can take place only under certain conditions and at certain restricted levels of the market, and in the second place because conversion is not reciprocal (it is possible to convert cultural capital into economic capital, but not vice versa). In the last instance symbolic and real capital are not equivalent, and this leaves open the question of the class location of intellectuals.

Now, Bourdieu posits that possessors of economic and cultural capital constitute two asymmetrical (dominant/dominated) fractions of the 'same' class. It is difficult, however – given that class is not defined in terms of *functional* identity – to know what establishes this sameness other than the assumed equivalence of the two forms of capital. Its effect is to bring about a systematically misleading conflation of the intelligentsia and its culture with the bourgeoisie and its culture – a conflation which is entirely the consequence of the initial methodological decision. Consider, for example, the histogram represented in figure 1. The class fractions are ranked in each case by educational capital, and this ranking establishes reasonably neat correlations between educational capital and musical preferences. If we rank the fractions by *economic* capital, however – with 'professions', 'secondary teachers', and 'higher-education teachers [and] art producers' slotted after 'cultural intermediaries [and] art craftsmen', and with 'industrial and commercial employers' moved to the top of the scale – the profiles look far less regular, as shown in figure 2. The sleight of hand by which the first histogram is organized – the substitution of an educational for an economic hierarchy – conceals the fact that, because of the specialized relationship of the intelligentsia to culture, there can be no immediate correlation of taste with class structure.

What Bourdieu does, in fact, is stress both the ideological incompatibility

1 *The Well-Tempered Clavier*	%	0	10	20	30	40	50	60
manual workers								
domestic servants	3							
craftsmen, shopkeepers	2							
clerical and commercial employees	1							
junior administrative executives	4.5							
junior commercial executives, secretaries	9							
technicians	10.5							
medical and social services	11							
primary teachers	7.5							
cultural intermediaries, art craftsmen	12.5							
industrial and commercial employers	4							
public-sector executives	5							
private-sector executives, engineers	14.5							
professions	15.5							
secondary teachers	31.5							
higher-education teachers, art producers	33.5							

2 *Rhapsody in Blue*								
manual workers	20.5							
domestic servants	3							
craftsmen, shopkeepers	20							
clerical and commercial employees	22							
junior administrative executives	27.5							
junior commercial executives, secretaries	26.5							
technicians	42							
medical and social services	20							
primary teachers	20							
cultural intermediaries, art craftsmen	22.5							
industrial and commercial employers	22.5							
public-sector executives	15							
private-sector executives, engineers	29							
professions	19							
secondary teachers	12.5							
higher-education teachers, art producers	12							

3 *'The Blue Danube'*								
manual workers	50.5							
domestic servants	35.5							
craftsmen, shopkeepers	49							
clerical and commercial employees	52							
junior administrative executives	34							
junior commercial executives, secretaries	29.5							
technicians	21							
medical and social services	15.5							
primary teachers	10							
cultural intermediaries, art craftsmen	12.5							
industrial and commercial employers	21.5							
public-sector executives	20							
private-sector executives, engineers	18.5							
professions	15.5							
secondary teachers	4							
higher-education teachers, art producers	0							

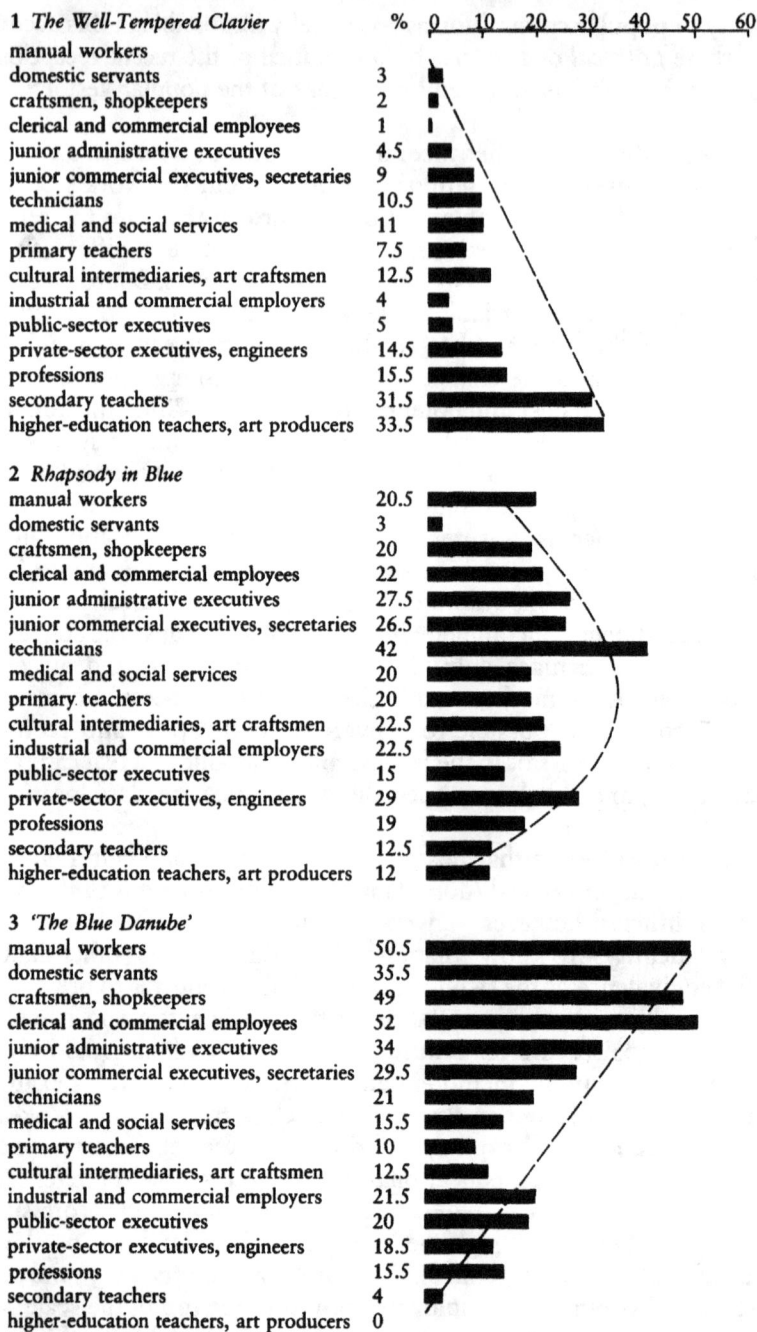

Figure 1. Distribution of preferences for three musical works by class fraction, ranked by educational capital

Source: Pierre Bourdieu, *Distinction: A Social Critique of the Judgement of Taste*, trans. R. Nice (Cambridge, Mass.: Harvard University Press, 1984), p. 17.

1 *The Well-Tempered Clavier*

	%	0 10 20 30 40 50 60
manual workers		
domestic servants	3	
craftsmen, shopkeepers	2	
clerical and commercial employees	1	
junior administrative executives	4.5	
junior commercial executives, secretaries	9	
technicians	10.5	
medical and social services	11	
primary teachers	7.5	
cultural intermediaries, art craftsmen	12.5	
professions	15.5	
secondary teachers	31.5	
higher-education teachers, art producers	33.5	
public-sector executives	5	
private-sector executives, engineers	14.5	
industrial and commercial employers	4	

2 *Rhapsody in Blue*

	%	
manual workers	20.5	
domestic servants	3	
craftsmen, shopkeepers	20	
clerical and commercial employees	22	
junior administrative executives	27.5	
junior commercial executives, secretaries	26.5	
technicians	42	
medical and social services	20	
primary teachers	20	
cultural intermediaries, art craftsmen	22.5	
professions	19	
secondary teachers	12.5	
higher-education teachers, art producers	12	
public-sector executives	15	
private-sector executives, engineers	29	
industrial and commercial employers	22.5	

3 *'The Blue Danube'*

	%	
manual workers	50.5	
domestic servants	35.5	
craftsmen, shopkeepers	49	
clerical and commercial employees	52	
junior administrative executives	34	
junior commercial executives, secretaries	29.5	
technicians	21	
medical and social services	15.5	
primary teachers	10	
cultural intermediaries, art craftsmen	12.5	
professions	15.5	
secondary teachers	4	
higher-education teachers, art producers	0	
public-sector executives	20	
private-sector executives, engineers	18.5	
industrial and commercial employers	21.5	

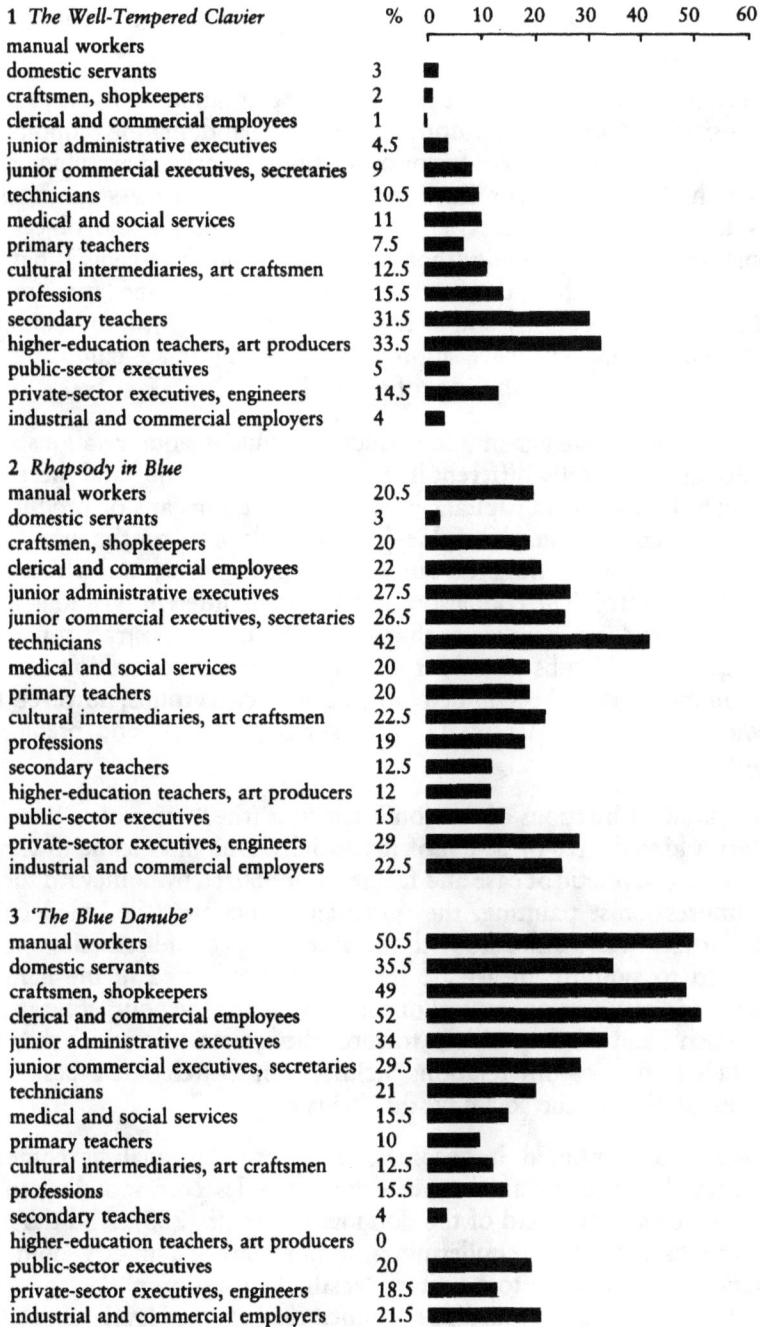

Figure 2. Distribution of preferences of class fractions, ranked by economic capital

and the underlying class unity of the intelligentsia and the bourgeoisie. Thus he writes:

> Through the mediation of the means of appropriation available to them, exclusively or principally cultural on the one hand, mainly economic on the other, and the different forms of relation to works of art which result from them, the different fractions of the dominant class are oriented towards cultural practices so different in their style and object and sometimes so antagonistic (those of 'artists' and 'bourgeois') that it is easy to forget that they are variants of the same fundamental relationship to necessity and to those who remain subject to it, and that each pursues the exclusive appropriation of legitimate cultural goods and the associated symbolic profits. (p. 176)

But again this is a sleight of hand, since the 'fundamental relationship to necessity' is structurally different in each case. On the one hand there is an investment of economic capital, a control over the means of production, and an extraction of surplus value from a workforce; on the other hand there is a position of wage labour or self-employment, and a delegated function of control. The conflation of these quite different positions in the relations of production indicates that something like an abstract concept of 'privilege' has been substituted for any more rigorous conception of class.

It is on the basis of the assumed unity of these two groups, however, that Bourdieu can then differentiate their systems of aesthetic preference. Whereas

> the dominant fractions of the dominant class (the 'bourgeoisie') demand of art a high degree of denial of the social world and incline towards a hedonistic aesthetic of ease and facility, symbolized by boulevard theatre or Impressionist painting, the dominated fractions (the 'intellectuals' and 'artists') have affinities with the ascetic aspect of aesthetics and are inclined to support all artistic revolutions conducted in the name of purity and purification, refusal of ostentation and the bourgeois taste for ornament; and the dispositions towards the social world which they owe to their status as poor relations incline them to welcome a pessimistic representation of the social world. (p. 176)

The more differentiated it becomes, the more this analysis comes to emphasize the antagonism 'between the life-styles corresponding to the opposing poles of the field of the dominant class' (p. 283). And the more this is the case, the more it undermines the postulate of a unitary 'dominant aesthetic' corresponding to a unitary 'aesthetic disposition'.

In the same way, Bourdieu's unification at the level of capital-equivalence of a 'dominant class' leads him to neglect the potential for contradiction in the role of the intelligentsia. The coincidence between the voting patterns of intellectuals and the working class seems to him 'paradoxical' (p. 438), and contradictions in political ideology are read as a sign of bad faith – in this passage, for example:

The members of the intellectual occupations (teachers, researchers, artists) declare themselves, more often than all other categories, 'supporters of revolutionary action', opposed to 'authoritarianism' and in favour of 'international class solidarity'. . . . But their answers often betray an ethos at variance with their discourse: they say more often than manual workers that their 'confidence in the trade unions' has declined since May 1968 or that an individual's most important characteristic is his personality (manual workers more often cite class) or that 'economic progress has benefited the majority' (workers more often think it has only benefited a minority). It may be that the tendency to political hyper-coherence which leads intellectuals to treat every problem as political and to seek perfect coherence in all attitudes in all areas of life is imposed on them by the fundamental discrepancy between their ethos and their discourse, especially when they originate from the dominated fractions of the dominant class. (pp. 420–1)

The disparity between 'ethos' and 'discourse' is taken as an index of hypocrisy, and Bourdieu goes on to cite the 'nuances' of expression – evident only in the interview situation and too subtle to be reproduced in his text – which subvert the reality or the genuineness of these opinions. But the disparity could equally be read as a sign both of the possibility of contradiction within a class and within a class fraction (the intelligentsia has an unstable class location and is not itself unified), and of the power of cultural capital to motivate a partial break with the 'objective' determinants of class ethos and class condition. A different account of intellectuals – that of Poulantzas, for instance, who identifies the intelligentsia as a 'new petty bourgeoisie', or that of Wright, who stresses its contradictory class location[11] – would emphasize both the political ambivalence of the intelligentsia and the irreducibility of cultural capital to economic class.

The important point here is that, without a more complex analysis of the political and ideological functions of intellectuals, Bourdieu is unable to theorize relations of domination as relations of contested hegemony. Rather, he is forced to think in terms of a simple opposition between two discrete class and cultural formations. It is true that this rigid dichotomization is modified somewhat in later sections of the book: Bourdieu argues against the existence of an autonomous 'popular culture' and concludes that the urban working class 'remains fundamentally defined by the relation of dispossessed to possessor which links it to the bourgeoisie, in culture as in other areas' (p. 395); and he quotes Gramsci to support his argument that there are many features of the working-class lifestyle 'which, through the sense of incompetence, failure or cultural unworthiness, imply a form of recognition of the dominant values' (p. 386). But this dominance of the dominant values – which is never really given a historical and national specificity – then seems to become something absolute, and the working class to be inevitably and inexorably entrapped within the cultural limits imposed on it. Thus Bourdieu contends that 'the dominated, whose interests are bound up with the raising of consciousness, that is, with language, are at the mercy of the discourses that are presented to them; whenever they emerge from doxa they are liable to fall into allodoxia, into all the false recognitions encouraged by the dominant discourse' (p. 461); and even political insight is insufficient to break the hold of these false recognitions, since 'the most politically conscious fraction of the working class remains profoundly subject, in culture and language, to the dominant norms and values, and therefore deeply sensitive to the effects of authority imposition which every holder of cultural authority can exert' (p. 396). The totalizing grip of the 'dominant norms', understood as a unitary set of values, allows for no possibility of critique and social transformation.

Which makes it all the harder to understand what constitutes the possibility of Bourdieu's own critical exteriority to the dominant norms. Certainly it is not a *political* positioning which would inscribe its own class interest in the analysis, since Bourdieu detaches his categories from the political process. Nor is it given in the disrupted and ambivalent situation of the intelligentsia. One can only conclude that it is a purely philosophical, that is a purely *disciplinary*, authority that enables Bourdieu's work to stand outside and above the game of intellectual competition, outside the political imaginary, outside the categories of a dominant and all-embracing culture. Thus, writing of the specular dialectic of boulevard and avant-garde theatre, Bourdieu remarks that 'the whole process constitutes a perfect circle from which the only escape is to objectify it sociologically' (p. 235). It is the regime of truth ordering the discipline of *sociology* that yields the single point of exception to the 'labour of domination' (p. 511) performed by all (other) intellectual work, and that allows Bourdieu to make the triumphal claim that his book has 'produced the truth of the taste against which, by an immense repression, the whole of legitimate aesthetics has been constructed' (p. 485). Written from an *impossible* perspective, a point that transcends the social space, *Distinction* ends up like the king in medieval social taxonomy, 'who, by setting himself up as the absolute subject of the classifying operation, as a principle external and superior to the classes it generated (unlike the three orders, who were subjects but also objects, judges but also parties), assigned each group its place in the social order, and established himself as an unassailable vantage-point' (p. 477).

Murdoch University, Perth, Western Australia.

Notes

1 Pierre Bourdieu, *Distinction: A Social Critique of the Judgement of Taste* (1979), trans. R. Nice (Cambridge, Mass.: Harvard University Press, 1984), p. 6. Further references to this will appear in the text as page numbers in parentheses.
2 Pierre Bourdieu and Alain Darbel, *L'Amour de l'art: les musées d'art européens et leur public*, 2nd rev. edn (Paris: Minuit, 1969), p. 69.
3 The sociology of language is treated at greater length in Pierre Bourdieu, *Ce*

que parler veut dire: l'économie des échanges linguistiques (Paris: Fayard, 1981).

4 Pierre Bourdieu and J.-C. Passeron, *Reproduction in Education, Society and Culture* (1970), trans. R. Nice (London: Sage, 1977), p. 25.

5 There is a more mediated version of this model in Bourdieu's frequent practice of reading texts as expressive of the dispositions of authors and then reducing authors to the class positions they represent; for example, 'Differences between works are predisposed to express differences between authors, partly because, in both style and content, they bear the mark of their authors' socially constructed dispositions (that is, their social origins, retranslated as a function of the positions in the field of production which these dispositions played a large part in determining)' (p. 20). More generally, Bourdieu tends to reduce all intellectual practice to the figures of intellectuals and the play of their career interests in a closed intellectual market. He thereby minimizes both the overdetermination of this market by other social forces, and the *ideological* positions – the truth-values – that intellectuals put in play. See Pierre Bourdieu, 'Intellectual field and creative project', in M. Young (ed.), *Knowledge and Control: New Directions for the Sociology of Education* (London: Collier Macmillan, 1971), pp. 161–88; 'Les fractions de la classe dominante et les modes d'appropriation des œuvres d'art', *Information sur les sciences sociales*, 13, 3 (1974); 'The specificity of the scientific field and the social conditions of the progress of reason', *Social Science Information*, 14, 4 (1975), pp. 19–47; and David Turnbull, 'Pierre Bourdieu and the Blainey debate', *Arena*, 74 (1986), pp. 133–7.

6 Pierre Bourdieu, L. Boltanski, R. Castel and J.-D. Chamboredon, *Un Art moyen: essai sur les usages sociaux de la photographie* (Paris: Minuit, 1965), pp. 25, 48.

7 Bourdieu and Darbel, op. cit., p. 73.

8 Ibid., p. 81.

9 See Gareth Stedman Jones, *Languages of Class: Studies in English Working Class History, 1832–1982* (Cambridge: Cambridge University Press, 1983); Paul Willis, *Learning to Labour: How Working Class Kids Get Working Class Jobs* (Farnborough: Saxon House, 1977); Richard Sennett and Jonathan Cobb, *The Hidden Injuries of Class*, 2nd edn (New York: Vintage, 1973).

10 See, for example, Nicholas Garnham and Raymond Williams, 'Pierre Bourdieu and the sociology of culture', *Media, Culture and Society*, 23, 3 (1980), pp. 209–23.

11 Nicos Poulantzas, *Political Power and Social Classes* (1968), trans. T. O'Hagan (London: New Left Books/Sheed & Ward, 1973); Erik Olin Wright, 'Intellectuals and the class structure of capitalist society', in Pat Walker (ed.), *Between Labour and Capital* (Boston, Mass.: South End Press, 1979).

A NEW JOURNAL
OF THE PLAGUE YEAR

> This may serve a little to describe the dreadful condition of
> that day, though it is impossible to say anything that is able
> to give a true idea of it to those who did not see it, other
> than this, that it was indeed very, very, very dreadful, and
> such as no tongue can express.[1]

O
n 19 January 1900, 33-year-old Mr A.P., 'a rather slight muscular
man, fair and of nervous temperament', was driving a lorry
through the city of Sydney at about noon when he was suddenly
seized with giddiness, headache and stomach pain. When he had
delivered his load to the warehouse, he lay down for a while, but continued
with his work in the afternoon 'though still suffering'. His condition
deteriorated overnight, and on 25 January he was positively diagnosed as
suffering from bubonic plague.[2]

The official medical report does not tell us whether or not A.P. died;
after 24 January, attention shifts from A.P. to the condition of the mice and
guinea pigs injected with tissue specimens from his infected glands. These
very rapidly developed the plague and were dead within a day, and the
medical report then concerned itself with the results of the post-mortems
(complete with photographs of dissected animals).

During the months that followed the diagnosis of A.P.'s illness, 303
confirmed cases of plague were found in the Sydney metropolitan area,
with 103 people dying. There was panic among sections of the population,
and crowds besieged the Queen Victoria building demanding inoculations;
serum was in short supply and had to be brought from Noumea – one of
the ports regarded as the point of origin of the Sydney outbreak. Reports
claimed that many people fled to the Blue Mountains to escape.[3]

This panic relates more to the symbolic power which the plague has in
the European imagination, rather than to the size of any real threat which it
posed the population of Sydney at the time. (This is not to argue at all that
no threat was posed, but simply to suggest that fear of disease owes more
to the social meanings of that disease; for example, the current instance of
AIDS and the hysteria it has caused owes relatively little to the actual threat
that it poses and much more to the linking of the disease with particular
social groups – homosexuals, prostitutes, drug addicts. In a similar way,
the outbreak of bubonic plague in Sydney at the turn of the century caused
alarm because it was linked with the Chinese and the working class.)

This outbreak of plague in Sydney at the time of Federation provides a useful reference point for a consideration of the development and operations of local power, first in a colony and then in a new nation-state. In order to examine these questions I shall refer to a 'document' produced in the aftermath of the plague – a set of photographs, produced under the directions of a Public Works Department consultant engineer, George McCredie. The Sydney plague photographs record the clean-up operations following the plague outbreak, and they are an important document in the development of the institutional discourses of public health and town planning, which in turn give rise to the privatized dreams of suburban Australia. It needs to be noted here, however, that the plague is by no means the beginning-point of the suburban dream, but rather the end of a process, since throughout the last quarter of the nineteenth century those residential areas of inner Sydney which were most affected by the plague had been gradually rezoned for business use, so that the plague provided a much-needed pretext for removing those sections of the working-class population who stood in the way of the progress envisaged by the city fathers.

The photographs themselves constitute a sort of imagery of horror and abjection, akin to the work of Jacob Riis in New York slums, also at the turn of the century, and similar to many other photographs produced in urban centres around the world at a time when a middle-class fascination for 'how the other half lives' was most pronounced. Photography played a quite crucial role in providing the evidence needed to justify the implementation of a certain social policy – or 'policing' of the population.[4]

The Sydney plague photographs do not, however, present subjects as objects; they are not portraits of slum residents but, rather, portraits of buildings and streets. They belong, therefore, within the genre of landscape rather than portraiture. Aside from two or three gruesome photographs of rat-catchers, piles of dead rats and the 'rat incinerator', the images represent horror and abjection *by implication only*. The photographs do not *show* us the horror of plague but function more as a rhetorical device which evokes abjection by withholding the description of it. To this extent, the photographs might be seen to operate in the same way in which Defoe's *writing* operates in a similar instance:

> it is impossible to say anything that is able to give a true idea of it to those who did not see it, other than this, that it was indeed very, very, very dreadful, and such as no tongue can express.[5]

I wish here to examine the process by which the photographs obtain their power to function in this way. I am not arguing that it is the 'verbal'/discursive alone which determines the possible readings of the photographs. In placing these images in the genre of landscape, I am suggesting that a certain history of representation since the Renaissance is another of the determinants of photographic meaning – one which might be called the 'visual'/discursive. Specifically, what has to be accounted for is the process that separates out particular images/landscapes of urban environments and presents them as being instances of social problems rather than works of art. This division within landscape becomes extreme in the nineteenth century with the development of photography – described by Steiglitz as 'the bastard child of Science and Art'.

While the principles of monocular perspective provide, on one level, the means for reading photographs, it is only with developments in realism – which might be said to have both a 'visual'/discursive and a 'verbal'/discursive dimension – and the development of empirical science (including, especially, the social 'sciences') that certain readings of images become possible.

The state's response to the plague in Sydney is very interesting as an instance of a certain consciousness of the threat which sections of the population (rather than the disease itself) posed. The clean-up operations which were instigated after the outbreak consisted of what can only be seen as an extremely violent attempt to cleanse the city not only of an unwanted disease but also of its unwanted population. Chloride of lime, carbolic, sulphuric acid and limewash were used in large amounts to cleanse vast areas of the inner city, east of Darling Harbour. Indeed, it was reported that the fish in Darling Harbour were killed in the process. There was criticism of the over-enthusiasm with which the cleansing operations were conducted. Peter Behrendt, a German-trained architect and engineer, objected to what he regarded as a reckless waste of disinfectants – only to be sacked from his position because of complaints that he was 'too economical'.[6]

In addition to the cleansing operations, buildings were demolished in what was, in effect, an *ad hoc* slum-reclamation programme. These houses and buildings were mostly in the inner-city areas where slums had existed since the mid-nineteenth century – areas occupied by what were regarded as 'the lower classes'. By the late 1850s these inner-city slums were already a cause for some alarm (as evidenced by the 1859–60 Legislative Assembly Select Committee Inquiry into the Condition of the Working Classes of the Metropolis, chaired by Henry Parkes).

Views taken during cleansing operations

But it was a public good that justified the private mischief.[7]

To document the clean-up operations, George McCredie, the consultant engineer in charge of the operations, ordered that photographs be taken. These photographs provided documentary evidence that a job had been done, but, more importantly perhaps, they were intended to be used as evidence *in case litigation arose*. So, although it is difficult to find evidence of the existence of *resistance* to the *ad hoc* slum-reclamation programme which the plague justified, there is, within the bureaucratic imagination and the decisions it made, evidence that resistance existed.

Over 400 photographs were taken. Collected in six volumes, the images, which are uncaptioned except by their locations, represent what might be seen as a shorthand account of the plague. However, the photographs in themselves tell us very little; they do not contain engaging portraits of the poor; they are not composed as artistic landscapes with attention to lighting or the rules of 'good' composition; they are taken by a government photographer, a public servant, working under the directions of an engineer. The question who the photographer was (which, at any rate, has been answered) is hardly relevant to a consideration of images like these. Any attempt to identify a personal style or to attribute authorship in this case may well satisfy the needs of a certain historiography, but the value of the photographs lies elsewhere.

In order to read the images, it is necessary to go to the official government medical report, which together with the photographs provides maps, not only of the extent of a feared disease, but also of the extent of official knowledge about the population of the time. In this work I am not so much concerned with the empirical details of the plague (and its background in nineteenth-century Sydney) as with the meanings which it had for the population at the time (or, more particularly, those sections of the population which were able to determine public opinion and policy). I am not, therefore, using the empirical details as facts which provide evidence but rather am pointing to the ways in which those facts and evidence were themselves *products* of a particular methodology and world-view.

Histories

Several histories intersect with the plague and its various 'outbreaks' at the turn of the century. First, there is the history of 'public health' and its relation to the development of quarantine regulations – designed as much with the effect on trade as with public health in mind. In the nineteenth century the debates on public health were closely involved with debates on free trade and protectionism (in spite of an ordering of knowledges which would clearly separate the two). During that period the establishment of public health departments took place at the same time as international conferences to reach agreement about quarantine regulations. For example the New South Wales Department of Public Health was brought into existence by the 1896 Public Health Act. In 1897, an international conference on plague was held in Venice to discuss means of controlling the spread of the dreaded disease (in ways which would not unduly affect trade).

Second, and closely related to this first history, there is a history of literature and the place which plague has within this, a history which is not only about medicine but also about the ways in which illness and disease function as metaphors. For example, Defoe's highly moral *Journal of the Plague Year*, published in 1722 and ostensibly documenting the 1665 plague outbreak in London; Camus's *La Peste* (1947), in which the dreaded disease functions as a commentary on a political situation. Relevant to this consideration are the ways in which the literary has been inscribed within writing styles not usually regarded as 'literary' – i.e. social description.

Third, there is a history of town planning and the establishment of the state's role in the ordering of urban space in the nineteenth century. It is in the nineteenth century that the need to order and regulate urban space arises; building regulations are instigated, and official inquiries held into living conditions.

Fourth, there is the history of photography as an instrument assisting other disciplines. Attempts to write photography's history have tended to lay down its pedigree in terms of art – always regarded as a privileged use of the photographic over its more prosaic commercial or scientific uses. However, the real *power* of photography lies precisely in these other areas, where photography's relation to other forms of power is much more blatant – if masked precisely by this privileging of the innocent art photograph produced under artisanal conditions.

Photography's Acquisition of Speech

If photography can be said to speak for itself, how does this come about? What language does it use?

In their standard history of photography,[8] Alison and Helmut Gernsheim tell us that the first documentary photographs were used to provide images for Henry Mayhew's *London Labour and the London Poor* (1861–2), a mammoth sociological work deriving its power from its claims to truth and authenticity. Mayhew's work first appeared in the London *Morning Chronicle* in 1849–50, and it is sparingly illustrated by woodcuts made from daguerreotypes by Richard Beard.

Thackeray wrote of Mayhew's work that it provides us with 'a picture of human life so awful, so piteous and pathetic, so exciting and terrible that readers of romances own they never read anything like to it.'[9] His comment points to the way in which Mayhew's work extends a blurring of the lines between the fictional and the factual which can be seen in Defoe's writing – a style which itself instigates a certain game with truth and authenticity, the potential of which is not realized until the nineteenth century. Whereas Defoe's journalistic account is known to be fictional, Mayhew's work derives its power from its claims to being factual; it belongs within a style of first-person reportage which, in Defoe's case, is clearly seen to be *literary*. However, by the nineteenth century, this style was no longer the monopoly of literature but had been appropriated by science (or, more particularly, by the newly developing social sciences). Mayhew's writing is above all literary rather than scientific, but it owes its power as truth to the belief that his observations on the working class were firsthand and real. By contrast with Dickens (to whom Mayhew might also be compared), the work was documentary rather than fiction.

It was, however, the illustrations which helped to secure the authenticity and truth-value of Mayhew's opus. The belief that photography was 'the pencil of nature'[10] meant that Mayhew's *writing* could be endowed with authority. He had seen with his own eyes that which he described and the proof of it was to be seen in the illustrations.

Mayhew's work begins with a peculiarly nineteenth-century attitude posing as sociological fact:

> Of the thousand millions of human beings that are said to constitute the population of the entire globe, there are – socially, morally and perhaps even physically considered – but two distinct and broadly marked races, viz., the wanderers and the settlers – the vagabond and the citizen – the nomadic and the civilized tribes.[11]

He then begins his attempt to classify:

> Those who obtain their living in the streets of the metropolis are a very large and varied class: indeed the means resorted to in order 'to pick up a crust' as the people call it, in the public thoroughfares (and such in many instances it *literally* is,) are so multifarious that the mind is long baffled in its attempts to reduce them to scientific order or classification.[12]

The 'scientific' approach of Mayhew's descriptive attempts is at every stage subverted by his own literariness. For example, in the following description which introduces a long story about the life of a coster lad, the detail which is given belongs almost entirely to the literary rather than the scientific:

> His two heavy lead-coloured eyes stared unmeaningly at me, and, beyond a constant anxiety to keep his front lock curled on his cheek, he did not exhibit the slightest trace of feeling. He sank into his seat heavily and of a heap, and when once settled down he remained motionless, with his mouth open and his hands on his knees – almost as if paralysed. He was dressed in all the slang beauty of his class, with a bright red handkerchief and unexceptional boots.
>
> 'My father', he told me in a thick unimpassioned voice, 'was a waggoner, and worked on the country roads . . .'[13]

This means of describing (and thereby producing) abjection has mobilized photography from its beginnings. The tradition is continued in, for example, James Agee's and Walker Evans's *Let Us Now Praise Famous Men*, perhaps the most classic of those texts which combine the literary and the photographic.

'Here we are in New South Wales' (words of a 19th c. popular song)

Engels's *Condition of the Working Class in England in 1844* provides a particular critical model for a style of social description of which Mayhew's work is another instance, albeit one which explains society in terms of the 'natural' foibles of individuals. At roughly the same time as Mayhew's book was published, its concerns were also those of liberal social reformers in the colony of New South Wales.

After the discovery of gold in the early 1850s, which produced only

266

poverty for large numbers of individual prospectors, depression gripped the colony; emancipated convicts, failed gold diggers and the unemployed were crowded together in Sydney, a city ill equipped to cope with its rapidly expanding population. The deterioration of sections of the city did not escape the attention of politicians and, under the initiative of Henry Parkes, a select committee was established to consider the condition of the working class of the metropolis.

This report might be seen as a key document in explaining why the Sydney plague photographs were taken forty years later. Other equally relevant official reports might be cited here, such as the 1876 *Report into Common Lodging Houses* or the report of the 1871 Royal Commission into the Chinese, but the Select Committee Report of 1859–60 has been chosen because the language it uses, in the Chairman's Report and in its style of questions and answers, cogently demonstrates the *graphic* quality of the description, and it is this style which paves the way for the use of photography at a later date.

The Select Committee of the Legislative Assembly to Consider the Conditions of the Working Classes was convened in September 1859 under the chairpersonship of the eminent parliamentarian, social reformer, poet and writer, Henry Parkes. (Parkes is also a major figure in the moves towards Federation which gathered momentum in the last quarter of the nineteenth century.) Its terms of reference were to take evidence and report on the *social* condition of the working class in relation to: the number of labourers and mechanics unemployed and the length of their unemployment; wage rates for 1857–9; 'the class of house accommodation in its moral and sanitary relations, and the number of freehold dwellings occupied by working mechanics and labourers'; the extent of 'juvenile vagrancy'.

The committee was also asked to consider one of Parkes's pet projects – the feasibility of establishing a nautical school for boys – as well as a number of other social concerns which Parliament had considered in the 1850s, such as the evidence of an 1854 Select Committee on Destitute Children and an 1854–5 Select Committee Report on the Increase of Intemperance.

The committee met twenty-two times and examined forty-one witnesses, who were asked a series of questions relating to the terms of reference. It recommended that regulations be introduced to ensure ventilation, sufficient space and conveniences for all dwellings and common lodging houses; the establishment of public bath and washhouses; public awards for building suitable houses; the appointment of a government health officer; the establishment of reformatory schools for 'vagrant children'; a wise and comprehensive system for settling industrious families on public lands; revision of the taxation system – and cautious support for a system of industry assistance as trade protection. Its final recommendation was that a government scheme be implemented to employ some of the unemployed in building a model group of workmen's cottages 'as an example to private capitalists'. This was in line with philanthropic thinking elsewhere in relation to the problems of housing the working class.[14] The select committee's recommendations went the way of many such official responses to living conditions. The 1900 plague outbreak indicated the extent to which these reasonable recommendations had not been implemented, forty years later.

Throughout the report there was particular concern with the moral condition of the working class; the committee concluded that, on the whole, housing was 'intolerably bad', but that 'the labouring masses of society' were of 'a high character for honesty, intelligence and sobriety'. The level of unemployment was taken to be real, yet the factor of people's 'lazy, idle habits' is constantly raised, so that it is possible to read within the responses to the evidence a certain fear of those sections of the population under observation for the purposes of the report.

This fear – and distaste – was in part produced by the very structure of the committee and its methods. In the official report, there is no evidence that the committee itself, as a whole, visited the areas under scrutiny. Individual witnesses certainly did, and some of these were committee members, but the 'working classes' are represented conspicuously by their absence. None of the witnesses belonged to the class under scrutiny: *the evidence consists entirely of reports from outside observers*. Some of these reports are extremely graphic, and my concern in this discussion of the report is with the style and language of the witnesses' accounts rather than with the content of them.

I am arguing that these descriptions have a *literary* quality akin to the style of realist fiction and that this descriptive style, because it is so graphic, paved the way for the use of photography in describing a range of new social subjects, brought into existence in the nineteenth century by new discursive forms.

Parkes presents a general description of housing in language which evokes abjection in a classical sense:

> A block of twenty or twenty-five wretched hovels affords shelter for perhaps a hundred human beings. The rooms, two in number are ten or eleven feet square and scarcely high enough for a man to stand erect; the floor is lower than the ground outside; the rain comes in through the roof and filth of all kinds washes in at the door; the court or yard, that is common to all, is covered with pollution that must be endured by all; and inside and out, everything is an object of disgust and wears a look of loathsomeness that would terrify men away, if it were possible to meet with its resemblance not familiarised to their senses through being created by themselves.[15]

High rents produced overcrowding which resulted in cases where '315 Chinamen are lodged in one building'. There are numerous 'haunts of vice and promiscuous association' – and the committee is especially concerned to hear descriptions of this, and of the moral condition of the occupants. Women, 'the weaker members of the abject household', are led to neglect their children, who are 'allowed to expose themselves to the sun'. There is a particular fascination with children on the part of the committee members and witnesses, all of whom are identified as 'family men', which heightens the horror of what they see: 'The streets are infested by a large number of vagrant children, or children entirely neglected by their parents, and some of the revelations of juvenile depravity are appalling and almost incredible.' The report does not specify in any more detail the exact nature of this reported 'appalling depravity', so that again abjection is evoked by the withholding of an actual description.

The first of the witnesses to the committee is the Inspector-General of Police, who is called to present evidence three times. Police opinion was sought because it was assumed that the police were the best authorities on the working class. The first witness's evidence in a sense provides the descriptive framework for the forging of a link between the working class and criminality. Questions such as 'Do you find particular trades affording a larger amount of criminals than others?' beg certain responses. Conveniently, the Inspector-General is able to provide the correct answer in the context of the inquiry – labourers.

There is also a particular concern to discover if any political organization exists among the unemployed in their attempts to resist cuts in daily rates. In spite of unemployment, the committee heard many reports that labourers would refuse to work for less than a certain minimum rate, which led them to suggest that perhaps there was some trade-union activity. In police and other witnesses' reports of meetings of the unemployed no distinction is made between political and criminal 'combination'; meetings of the unemployed are not regarded as politically motivated but as combinations of troublemakers bent on criminal intent.

Parkes, in his final report, refers to 'the darkening mass of physical and moral disease' and to this 'disordered state of things which is fast undermining the social happiness of the community', while at the same time arguing that the threat is limited to relatively small numbers.

It is useful to remember that Parkes was also a literary man, a poet and writer, as well as a politician, and that the style of the report owes much to this. However, he was also a social reformer, a man with a scientific concern for social conditions, and a belief in the validity of his own high moral values. The society which he, and other like-minded men, wished to bring about, a society in which individual liberty was the highest good, was dependent on the existence of citizens who shared the same principles.

Europe at the time was faced with similar fears of the masses. The uncontrolled expansion of Sydney and the inherent dangers this presented was therefore of particular concern to those who had escaped the Old World but knew of the threat of mob violence in the cities of England and Europe. So any demonstration that similar threats existed in the new colony was viewed with considerable concern, as presenting, indeed, 'dark features' which were undesirable however small in extent.

One of the means of dealing with this threat is to attempt to remove the problem – by suggesting that the population be encouraged to go 'into the interior', an option which the committee returns to time and time again. The reluctance on the part of the unemployed to go to the country is explained in terms of bad treatment, bad conditions, isolation and the impossibility of making any social progress in the country because of the way in which the lands had already been locked by squatters.

The second witness before the committee was a squatter, who recounts his own inadvertent efforts in discouraging the settlement of newcomers to the country by virtue of his higher bidding at a land auction. He was able to do this on account of his 'having 200 or 300 pounds to spare that day' (Minutes of Evidence, p. 9), so that the newcomers who had hoped to buy land were forced to return to the city and probable unemployment and poor living conditions. (Labourers at this time could not hope to earn more than £25 a year.) It is readily admitted by the committee that land laws needed changing, but difficult legislative change is dismissed in the face of what is seen to be the perversity of the working class. In the evidence of the Inspector-General of Police, 'A new arrival looks upon going to Ashfield as going into the bush' (Minutes of Evidence, p. 4). Ashfield was then a village less than 10 kilometres from Sydney.

The 'lower orders', were, throughout the nineteenth century, a source of fascination for the middle class and especially those sections of the professional middle class with an interest in the colonization of sectors of knowledge. Concerned private citizens interested in reform regularly toured working-class districts to enquire into 'social problems', especially prostitution and 'juvenile vagrancy'. These tours to discover evil were obsessive in their detail and involved the physical, bodily experience of revulsion.

Numerous witnesses referred to the evil smells encountered in these excursions into working-class neighbourhoods. This is found, for example, in a reply to question 228 of the Minutes of the Inquiry, 'On going to the door?' (of a two-roomed house occupied by twenty-five Chinese) – 'The smell is very offensive . . . I went home very ill after it' – and in the evidence of Henry Graham, city health officer:

> I have always observed in going in most nauseous and offensive effluvia from want of drainage and from over-crowding, particularly the latter; that peculiar foetor arising from the human body under such circum-stances being clearly distinguishable.

That the conditions under which people lived in slum districts were in part caused by the very moral attitudes of the highminded citizens who gave their opinions to the inquiry is not, of course, foregrounded (although the contradictions are noted by the more liberal of the committee members, such as Parkes). For example, in an amusing exchange between the committee and a Mr Clayton, city rate collector, it is learned that, for a time in the metropolis, street fountains were widespread. These provided a water supply for the poorer sections of the population and afforded washing facilities which were absent from the houses. The fountains were removed by the authorities, however, because they were considered to be meeting places for the unruly and the source of a rise in prostitution!

Q272. [To Clayton] Do you not think street fountains would be very advantageous in such neighbourhoods . . .? I may state that I recollect when we had street fountains here, and that they went a great way to increase prostitution in Sydney. When street fountains were about the town parents were too independent or too proud to go themselves or to send their children for water till after dark, and the consequence was that the girls formed a meeting place which led to improper intimacy. Some ten years back we had fountains all over the town. . . .

Q274. Then do you think pride in the city leads to prostitution? No doubt it goes a great way.

Perhaps the most graphic evidence presented to the inquiry is that of Harrison, a police inspector, and James Hugh Palmer, shorthand writer to the Legislative Assembly, who accompanied each other on nocturnal visits to the slums – and particularly to brothels. Harrison describes what he found on these visits:

Q377. . . . I was in about twenty brothels up to four o'clock this morning; I was looking after a party [consisting of Harrison, Palmer, another inspector of police and a 'private policeman'] and turned out a great number of prostitutes from the houses in Kent Street. One of the brothels I visited was kept by a black man, it has only one room and the flooring is a foot below the level of the lane; it has no drainage and everything is thrown out in the front. In this place, which is built of weatherboards, there were two beds; the landlord is a blackfellow, an old man of sixty years of age – he was lying on a mattress with an old barrowman; a girl and a sailor were lying in the same room, and behind a bit of a screen was a truckle bed with a woman on it, twenty-three or twenty-four years of age: she had been hocussed last Sunday – had some drug put into her drink by another inmate, a girl, for the purpose of stupifying her, and the drug had taken effect; she had never been out of her bed since Sunday and all she could take was a little cold water which her stomach rejected as fast as she drank it; she had not seen a doctor and was very ill; she had a child of about eighteen months old. On a mattress alongside the stretcher was a man who had been a sailor, and who has been knocking about Sydney for some time doing nothing; he said he was sleeping there for the night.

Palmer, the shorthand writer, not only gives his evidence but presents firmly held views about the object of his observations, when asked (Q1237) if he had taken particular notice of the inhabitants' physical health and moral condition:

I have. I may state that, as regards the general health of the people residing in the localities alluded to, it must be apparent to a very slight observer that the children to be found in the courts, lanes and alleys of the city, are in a much less healthy condition than those in the suburbs. I have no doubt the large rate of infantile mortality and disease which prevails in Sydney may be attributed to the want of ventilation in the houses, and of pure air in the streets. In some localities the stench arising from the cesspools and putrid matter collected in the water course of the street is so offensive as almost to overpower those who come from the purer air of the suburbs. This poisonous atmosphere must inevitably be peculiarly injurious to young children, induce diseases which we know to be prevalent here at certain seasons of the year, and where not attended with immediately fatal results deposit the seeds of much future physical debility and suffering. 'Impure air' says Mr Carmichael 'is one of the most powerful causes of scrofula'. . . . Consumption may also, I believe, be traced to the same cause; and as the children of consumptive and scrofulous parents are known to be generally precocious, I attribute in some measure to this the existence among the youth of this city, at so early an age of the desire for sexual intercourse.

I have quoted these witnesses at length to illustrate the graphic quality of the descriptions, which are typical of the evidence presented to many nineteenth-century inquiries into 'social problems'. Whereas it was firmly believed that these reports were 'objective' observations of real conditions, my point is that the *language* of the evidence resembles aspects of fiction more closely than reality. The select committee's report and many such government reports on 'social problems' in the nineteenth century were above all exercises in visualization (though not intentionally), exercises which demonstrated the existence of aspects of society previously invisible to the middle classes. These visualization exercises made it possible, by the end of the nineteenth century, to use photography, on its own, without all the words which multi-volumed inquiries used.

Photography could, finally, speak for itself, but largely because the graphic descriptive language which it depended on had already been placed in circulation.

Sydney College of the Arts.

Notes

This article is taken from material in an MA thesis-in-progress on the Sydney plague photographs. Photographs here are reproduced, with the permission of the New South Wales State Archives, from *Views Taken During Cleansing Operations, Quarantine Areas* (Sydney, 1900).

1 Daniel Defoe, *A Journal of the Plague Year* (1722; Harmondsworth: Penguin, 1966).

2 J. Ashburton-Thompson, MD, DPH, 'Report on plague', *Votes and Proceedings*, vol. 2 (New South Wales Government Printer, 1900).

3 Billy Hughes, quoted in Max Kelly, *Plague Sydney, 1900* (Sydney: Doak Press, 1981).

4 John Tagg, 'Power and photography: a means of surveillance: the photograph as evidence in law', *Screen Education*, 36 (Autumn 1980).

5 Defoe, op. cit.

6 Peter Behrendt, Petition to the Legislative Assembly, *Votes and Proceedings*, vol. 2 (New South Wales Government Printer, 1900).

7 Defoe, op. cit.

8 Alison and Helmut Gernsheim, *A Concise History of Photography* (London: Thames & Hudson, 1965), p. 166.

9 Henry Mayhew, *London Labour and the London Poor: A Cyclopaedia of the Condition and Earnings of Those That Will Work, Those That Cannot Work, and Those That Will Not Work* (London, 1861–2; New York: Dover, 1968), introduction by John D. Rosenberg.

10 A. and H. Gernsheim, op. cit., p. 81. 'The Pencil of Nature' is the title of W. H. Fox Talbot's book (1844) said to be the first ever photographically illustrated book.

11 Mayhew, op. cit., p. 1.

12 Ibid., p. 3.

13 Ibid., p. 39.

14 Enid Gauldie, *Cruel Habitations: A History of Working-Class Housing 1780–1918* (London: Allen & Unwin, 1974).

15 This and subsequent quotations are taken from the *Report of the Select Committee on the Condition of the Working Classes of the Metropolis, 1859–60* (New South Wales Government Printer, 1860).

MIKE EMMISON AND

ALEC McHOUL

DRAWING ON THE ECONOMY: CARTOON DISCOURSE AND THE PRODUCTION OF A CATEGORY

Introduction

T his article examines the changing form of representation which the economy – or that configuration of processes, institutions and practices which we readily subsume today under the category 'the economy' – has received in political cartoons from the early nineteenth century to the 1980s.

Terminological caution and precision are necessary prerequisites in this endeavour for, as we shall see shortly, in no sense could we be regarded as producing a 'cartoon history of the economy'.[1] To mention only one consideration, the modern concept of 'economy' itself is a relatively recent arrival on the scene, especially in cartoons. Further, it is crucial to our rethinking of its emergence as a category to realize that the discursive space which 'economy' now occupies was previously a quite different discursive space occupied by quite different categories – some of these, at least, being 'proto-economic' categories. Our aim in part is to chart these representational shifts and to account for their continuities and discontinuities.

Finally, by way of introduction it should be noted that, while our research draws overwhelmingly on cartoons from the British media, the inclusion of a number of examples from the United States and Australia can be justified, given our analytical concerns. That is, we are not so much interested in the national variations evident in the three countries' economic structures as in more fundamental economic conditions of possibility which they share as Western capitalist countries. In this sense it might be more accurate to view the cartoons not as nationally specific but as specific to particular transnational economic conjunctures.

The data corpus of cartoons we have selected begins with the early editions of *Punch* from the 1840s. While political and 'economic' cartooning certainly existed before this time, the ascendancy of *Punch* is still something of a watershed in cartooning history, given our interests. The world of 'high', 'serious' or, perhaps more appropriately, 'collectable' art had, without doubt, its great caricaturists, from Hogarth, through Rowlandson and Gillray, to Goya and Daumier. And a number of these had their political connections, particularly Daumier, who suffered imprisonment and persecution at the hands of those he lampooned. Yet the work of these early masters was inseparable from their 'serious' canvases and had, as its audience, those of bourgeoisie and the aristocrats, who could afford originals or, more likely, engravings.

By the early 1800s, however, printers could use cartoonists' direct drawings on wood blocks and juxtapose cartoons with regular print features. And it was only at this point that a specialized position within the division of labour for the cartoonist came about, so that popular cartooning became available to a relatively wide public for the first time. However, there is little doubt that a magazine such as *Punch* had, for its audience, a section of the critical bourgeoisie whose main object of ridicule was the remnants of the old landed gentry. George du Maurier, who succeeded the great *Punch* cartoonists John Leech and Charles Keene, identified his forebears as bohemians who saw the city as their natural habitat and who took the country pleasures of the aristocracy as little but objects of fun. Of Leech, probably Europe's first celebrated cartoonist (Millais and Dickens apparently wept 'like maidens' at his funeral), du Maurier writes:

> the only thing that he feared is the horse. Nimrod as he is, and the happiest illustrator of the hunting-field that ever was, he seems for ever haunted by a terror of the heels of that noble animal he drew so well – and I thoroughly sympathise with him.[2]

Leech and Keene, that is, were much more at home in the city of London, happier drawing cabbies, policemen, off-duty sailors and the grand bourgeoisie of Kensington than the landed aristocracy – except when the latter were at their most ridiculous, 'up in London'.

Leech, in particular, took his rightful place as the main political cartoonist for *Punch* – meaning that, aside from his regular duties as purveyor of 'social pictorial satire', he was given a page in each issue to address the political concern of the moment. This cartoon always had a blank page on its verso, perhaps so it could be cut from the magazine and passed from hand to hand without detriment to the stories. Whatever else its use, this weekly cartoon occupied a central place in the representation of English political life and, with some lean periods, rarely failed to produce comment of a (proto-)economic kind.

It is for these reasons that we select the early work of *Punch* as the first items of our corpus: it was the beginning of mass-produced cartoons of a kind; it involved a quite specialized and new division of labour; it saw the beginning of the spread of the cartoon form to a wider audience than the art-buying public; and it concentrated on urban life. Between its commencement in 1841 and the turn of the century, however, the social class composition of *Punch*'s object of satire, and presumably also its audience, changed quite markedly. Du Maurier, somewhat peeved at the earlier cartoonists' having the cream of the old aristocratic crop, complains in the last decade of the old century that these denizens of 'old England' are

> like the snows of yester-year! They have gone the way of their beautiful chariots with the elaborate armorial bearings and the tasselled hammer-cloth, the bewigged, cocked-hatted coachmen, and the two gorgeous flunkies hanging on behind. Sir Gorgeous Midas has beaten the dukes in mere gorgeousness, flunkies and all – burlesqued the vulgar side of them, and unconsciously shamed it out of existence; made swagger and ostentation unpopular by his own evil example – actually improved the manners of the great by sheer mimickry of their defects. He has married his sons and daughters to them and spoiled the noble curve of those lovely noses that Leech drew so well, and brought them down a peg in many ways, and given them a new lease of life; and he has enabled us to discover that they are not of such different clay from ourselves after all.[3]

On a class basis, then, the cartoons of *Punch*, during its first fifty or so years of publication, shifted their objects – and perhaps audience – to the new self-made middle class (enfranchised by 1868) and, half with admiration and half with nostalgia and distaste, plotted their installation into the seats of power.

Perhaps the most telling feature which the following analysis reveals is the relative absence of what we would now see as distinctively economic themes in nineteenth- and early twentieth-century cartoons, when compared with their omnipresence in today's media. Our argument is not that 'the economy' did not figure as a matter of pressing political concern (although such years *were* the heyday of British capitalism) but rather that the forms in which 'economic' issues were publicly conceived or debated were far more likely to be embedded within other discourses. Lacking any modern notion of an overall or aggregate economy, cartoons before the middle years of the twentieth century could only represent economic concerns in fragmented or 'local' (conjunctural) ways, subsumed for the most part within specifically political discourses.

Of equal interest, though at a different level of analysis, is the persistence of certain mythemic elements – nature/civilization, domestic order, the taming of brute forces and the like – which make their first appearance in the 'proto-economic' cartoons of the early nineteenth century. Although the elements themselves have persisted, it is their numerous forms of recombination in the later twentieth century, and therefore in the recent context of the aggregated economy, which has led to unique and cartoon-specific representations. Below, we trace both the ascendancy of the modern category of the economy and its representational elements and their recombinations.

Royal nursery rhymes

The first cartoon (figure 1) from 1843 shows clearly the dominance that 'the political' enjoyed, even when the matter at hand clearly touched upon economic issues. The sovereign Victoria, the 'Young Mother Hubbard', is represented as the ultimate arbiter over the matter of whether or not her politician dogs are fed. That is: whether or not they are allowed a diet of income tax to meet the impending bills and tariffs.

The setting is that familiar domestic one which comes increasingly in the proto-economic cartoons to represent safety and civilization as opposed to brute natural – including proto-economic – forces. In this cartoon, nature figures in the form of necessity, the food/income tax missing from the not quite empty cupboard. Civilization, national/domestic economic wellbeing, is portrayed as dependent on seemingly natural commodities which are in fact economic.

On the literal level, the cartoon diverges from (and gets its meaning from its divergence from) the paradigm nursery rhyme. The cupboard is not bare, but its filling by an economic negative (bills, tariffs) signifies a natural lack. In the middle of this contradiction, set between the sovereign arbiter and nature, is the state – the political dogs who are represented as both (or neither) natural and civilized, as domestic pets, dependent on both the beneficent Mother and the natural.

This cartoon, by representing the state as a dog with a human face, in fact prefigures the tendency of modern cartoons to use quite marked surrealist elements. In the later years of the nineteenth century, cartoons were to avoid this kind of visual pun in favour of a fairly strict realism, with the satire arising not so much from visual grotesqueries as from the relation between caption and quasi-realist drawing. It is also important to note that all parties – the sovereign, her pets, the narrator and the reader – have equal access to the 'real' (or natural) state of affairs. There is no hidden Real which explains the follies of state or royal policy. The situation is bare, plain and out in the open – on plain view – by contrast with some later and contemporary cartoons which use the opposite convention.

The overall effect of the cartoon is the presentation of a social and political arbitrary – income tax – as a natural formation. It presents the implementation of income tax legislation and policy as a natural step, as filling a natural lack just as food fills the natural space of hunger. The question of its status as social policy is overridden, forcefully forgotten in this form of representation. The mythemic elements of Nature, Civilization and their medial or synthetic types (the politician–dogs) are arranged so as to bring off this effect. The signs

> seem to say 'the object really *is* like this, your interpretant is formed by your experience of the object rather than by my sign. My sign is merely reminding you of, or is bringing you a reflection of, the object itself.'[4]

By contrast, fifty or so years later John Tenniel was to use much the same structure in his cartoon 'The Empty Cupboard' (figure 5), but clearly here

PUNCH'S PENCILLINGS.—N°. LIX.

ROYAL NURSERY RHYMES.

Young Mother Hubbard she went to the cupboard
To give her poor dog a bone ;
But when she got there the cupboard was bare,
And so the poor dog had none.

VOL. IV.—1843.

Figure 1

CARTOON, N° V.

CAPITAL AND LABOUR

Figure 2

PUNCH OR THE LONDON CHARIVARI.—February 2, 1895.

"MEAT! MEAT!"

H-SCH-L. "NOW LOOK 'ERE—YOU JUST WAIT YOUR TURNS—OR YOU'LL NONE OF YOU GET NOTHINK !"

Figure 3

PUNCH, OR THE LONDON CHARIVARI.—April 15, 1896.

NOT DONE YET.

MASTER ARTY B-LF-R (to MASTER BILL H-RC-T). "HA! YOU'VE BEEN PRETTY COCKY THIS HALF, BUT
WAIT TILL 'MY BIG BROTHER' GETS HOLD OF YER!"

Figure 4

SESSION 1895

THE EMPTY CUPBOARD.

OLD MOTHER HUBBARD SHE WENT TO THE CUPBOARD WHEN SHE GOT THERE THE CUPBOARD WAS BARE,
TO GET HER POOR DOG A BONE, AND SO THE POOR DOG HAD NONE.

[Mr. Chaplin, speaking in the House of Commons on the 19th August, said that it was not possible to prepare and produce measures for the relief of Agriculture this Session.—*Daily Paper.*]

Figure 5

HARCOURT'S FOOD for CATTLE

REVENUE

UNEARNED INCREMENT.

Sir M-ch-l H-cks-B-ch. "As, my hearty, if you keep petting me farms at this rate, we shall astonish them at the show!"
Farmer H-rc-t. "Yes! but they don't forget it's my food as has done it."

* The receipts into the Treasury, up to last Saturday, amounted to over five millions and a quarter more than in the corresponding period of the previous financial year, while the expenditure had but little increased.—*Daily Paper.*

Figure 6

THE TRUE ECONOMY.

John Bull (on the Territorials). "FINE SERVICE, WHAT? PITY THEY'RE SHORT OF MEN."
F.-M. Punch. "YES, MY FRIEND, AND IF YOU WANT YOUR VOLUNTARY SYSTEM TO GO
ON YOU'LL HAVE TO PUT YOUR HANDS A BIT DEEPER INTO YOUR POCKETS. YOU'LL
FIND IT CHEAPER IN THE END."

Figure 7

ECONOMIC LAW

UP AGAINST IT.

Capital to Labour. "YOU MAY SUCCEED IN KNOCKING ME OUT, BUT DON'T FORGET
THAT THEN YOU'LL HAVE TO FIGHT A CHAMPION THAT NO ONE CAN STAND UP
AGAINST."

Figure 8

the same elements are given quite different positions and values. In fact some of the elements are filled in ways which are in direct contradistinction to the 1843 version. In the place of the sovereign (although we shall see that this person is not quite off the scene by 1895) stands the figure of the state, who is now directly responsible for the provision of economic wellbeing (agricultural relief in this case). Far from being the pet to be fed, the state is now at the helm, and the position of domestic pet is taken up by an abstract economic fraction – agriculture – whereas before, in 1843, the economic concept was the food (or its lack) in the cupboard. The sovereign is absent, and the other elements have changed places. Yet the setting is still domestic and the plain or non-privileged point of view remains. Further, the surreal element of the earlier cartoon is missing. Apart from the necessary labelling of non-iconic symbols such as the cupboard and the dog, the scene is manifestly a visually possible one. The care and attention to detail of a quasi-realist kind is in marked contrast with the 1843 version, where many elements peripheral to the main focus are merely sketched, pencilled with a few simple strokes.

The attempt at artistic realism was a deliberate policy of the cartoonists of *Punch* at the turn of the century:

> I have always tried as honestly and truthfully as lies in me to serve up to the readers of *Punch* whatever I have culled with the bodily eye, after cooking it a little in the brain. . . . The people I meet seem to me more interesting than funny – so interesting that I am well content to draw them as I see them, after just a little arrangement and a very transparent disguise – and without any attempt to caricature.[5]

This aesthetic realism in the social sketches matched a philosophic realism of representation in the political/economic cartoons, for it was always real (rather than socially arbitrary) forces with which the relatively autonomous subjects in power had to deal. By representing concepts and formations, such as 'agriculture', as animals, they moved from being purely brute into being potentially domesticable. A kind of taming process was being suggested, then, by this circular shift of the cartoon's mythemic elements. And, thereby, the question of human agency was soon to be part of the agenda of the cartoonist.

Class and the body

In the 1840s and 1850s, the cartoon also kept very close to its original artistic position – as a paper sketch for the finished fresco (Italian *cartone*, 'paper'). And the magazines certainly made use of this type of cartoon also – a virtually captionless piece, grand in scale, often almost a blueprint or template portraying a wider version of the social world than the 'policy'-type economic and political cartoons. Also from 1843, then, we can turn to the *Punch* cartoon 'Capital and Labour' (figure 2), both for its contrast with the specificity of the earlier and later nursery rhymes because of this wider scale, and for its institutionalization of a continuing cartoon mytheme: the portrayal of class stereotypes.

While the side of Capital, the much smaller portion of the society, lives in luxury, even to the point where its children are waited on and its dogs sit on fine cushions, the greater proportion of the society are kept in a kind of cellar prison, cordoned off from Capital by a strong chain, the door guarded by a tough gaoler. While dogs sit on silk, men are forced into tiny coal seams which meander up to the surface, providing wealth and commodities for Capital. It is quite hard not to read here a version of a base/superstructure analysis of social relations of production and consumption – and that is certainly part of the representation. But further elements are at play. The location of the working class in the life of the body is an important one. They are seen to depend on the body for their labour and, in many cases, to suffer from physical deformities – thus to depend on the very thing which becomes weaker as it is used in the maintenance of life.

The remarkable thing about this cartoon and its type is that it never surfaces again in the history of popular cartoons. The wide-angle general vision, the lack of specificity, the non-attachment to a particular policy, topic or concept are replaced by a particularistic realism (in the early stages) and a form of return to caricature and surrealism (from the mid-1940s). However, the representation of relations between Capital, leisure and mental life, on the one hand, and Labour, toil and the body, on the other, remains.

The realist forms of representation that were characteristic of the proto-economic cartoons at the turn of the century are evident once more in 'Unearned Increment' (figure 6) and 'Meat! Meat!' (figure 3). In 'Unearned Increment', while the scene is no longer domestic, other elements arise to suggest a civilized setting – the tidy farmyard, well-dressed gentlemen and the pig bred for show rather than use. The 'revenue pig' also differs quite crucially from the typical use of animals in cartoons of the same period. Typically animals represented specific interest groups – 'the Welsh', 'Labour', 'agriculture' (figure 3) – while the pig constitutes an early attempt to represent an aggregate economic concern employing the categories that were then available. Research we have done elsewhere on historical shifts in economic discourse suggests that it was terms such as 'the revenue', 'the surplus' and the like which occupied the discursive space filled later by the category 'the economy'.[6] As we discuss below, the notion of an aggregate economic totality – a complex system of production, exchange and consumption, together with its assorted ills – did not emerge until the late 1930s. While not conveying precisely the same idea, the use of 'the revenue' was an attempt at the summation of national economic wellbeing by an overall fiscal measure.

The 'revenue pig' in this sense must be seen as a precursor to the snakes, dragons and assorted beasts that the aggregate economy assumed in cartoons of the post-Second World War period. Moreover, the pig is a comfortable and cosseted creature shown to be in the capable hands of the state – again a departure from many contemporary cartoons. Finally of interest here is the implied knowledge of those portrayed which is no longer equal and even. There is something which the pig's admirer has forgotten and which he has to be reminded of, ostensibly by Harcourt, but more clearly by the narrative voice of the cartoon itself. The cartoon, that is, has become less of a 'scene' or vignette and has become a kind of minor drama.

The last cartoon from this period is the 1895 'Not Done Yet' (figure 4). This piece is interesting, for it shows the disagreements between Balfour and Harcourt to be still predicated on the decisions of the sovereign who waits behind the wall, little interested as yet in their petty skirmishes. As we saw Harcourt in 'Meat! Meat!' transformed into a cockney butcher, we now see him brought down another metaphoric peg to the figure of the schoolboy – both of these steps signifying a fall away from the mature, the civilized and the controlled. What is most interesting about this cartoon is its structural similarity, and its differences on the plane of content, with a cartoon from 1921, 'Up Against It' (figure 8). In the latter we see the three characters in an almost identical pose – except perhaps that the champion is now decidedly more interested in the contest. However, substitutions have been made. In place of the sovereign stands Economic Law portrayed as a professional fighter. In the place of the political contenders from Westminster are ranged Capital and Labour once more.

We are still confronted with a political struggle, but now the content or substance of that struggle is decidedly 'economic' in content. The issue of wage cuts came to the forefront in the years following the First World War, culminating eventually in the General Strike of 1926. The reigning economic orthodoxy was that market forces would and must prevail and that labour should accept a wage reduction and become again 'employable'. Here we see these market forces anthropomorphized into the prize fighter Economic Law ready to step in on Capital's behalf should this be necessary. Plainly Labour is picking the fight, placing itself on the side of the body once more, while Capital is more reluctant to fight, showing discretion and admitting to weaknesses of the brute physical kind, thereby placing itself on the side of civilization and control. But the contenders are unequal, for Capital can call upon the assistance of a super-natural force that even the working class's stereotypical association with the body cannot easily overcome.

The main significance of this cartoon for our analysis lies in what it does *not* contain. The terrain has been shifted away from the proto-economic aggregates of two decades earlier and is now firmly located within a partial but then theoretically ascendant economic conception – that of the market forces of supply and demand. A concomitant of this is that the cartoon contains no space for the state. In this period of chronic economic crisis, the government remained quiescent and was able to legitimize its non-intervention by appealing to the prevailing neoclassical economic orthodoxy.

All this was to change with the Keynesian-inspired 'revolution' in

PUNCH, OR THE LONDON CHARIVARI — May 5, 1926.

A LARGE ORDER.

JOHN BULL. "WHO FAILED TO GET THIS TREE DOWN?"
WASHINGTON. "I WILL NOT TELL A LIE. WITH MY LITTLE HATCHET I HAVE FAILED TO MAKE MUCH IMPRESSION ON IT. BUT I PROPOSE TO CONTINUE THE GOOD WORK."

Figure 9

THE FRIGHT THAT FAILED

Figure 10

UNOFFICIAL STRIKE

Figure 11

ALL ABOARD
"Any more for the Leviathan?"

Figure 12

economic thinking in the 1930s. From this point on, the idea of an aggregated economic structure – 'the economy' – and the crucial role which the state should play within this totality of forces and processes, became the new focus of economic theory, a situation which was eventually translated into new forms of cartoon representation. It is important for our argument to understand clearly what was entailed by this shift in economic theory. It is not the case that Keynes 'discovered' the economy but rather that, in pointing out the implications of the existence of a national economic structure, he gave the term 'economy' a new and decisive meaning. The term was, of course, in currency long before Keynes but it always conveyed the older formal notion of 'economizing'. Economy, in this sense, was a state of affairs which rational actors should achieve by wise expenditure, careful budgeting and the like.[7]

This earlier meaning can be clearly seen in two cartoons published prior to the 1930s, both of which invoke the category of economy. For example, the subject matter of 'The True Economy' (figure 7) from 1910 bears no relation to the aggregate economic structure. Instead it is the classical notion of econom*izing* – necessary but prudent expenditure – which is being raised and urged upon John Bull: 'You'll have to put your hands a bit deeper into your pockets. You'll find it cheaper in the end.'

Similarly in 'A Large Order' (figure 9) from 1926 the theme of economizing reappears, this time in the form of cutting back unnecessary spending. John Bull is now shown as having grasped these elementary principles and is taking Churchill to task for his failure to curb 'excessive expenditure', his axe – 'economy' – having made little impression on the vast tree trunk.

The emergence of the modern usage for 'economy' is bound up with the rejection in the 1930s – which owes much to Keynes – of the assumptions of neoclassical theory.[8] Keynes argued convincingly that the economic wellbeing of a nation could be vastly improved by the then heretical notion of acting in ways that had previously been considered *un*economical. The economic orthodoxy of the 1920s and 1930s, with its divination of the laws of supply and demand, could only conceive of individual economic agents, be they firms or people, subject to the market mechanism. Keynes's suggestion was that there existed a level of economic analysis other than this, in fact a national economic structure that was capable of being, and indeed should be, modified by government action. To facilitate the expression of this idea he begins to refer to 'the economy' as a totality, as something more than the combined activity of the individual economic units. While the Keynesian revolution in economic thinking cannot be reduced to a minor change in terminology, a change in linguistic usage was a necessary feature of the ideas he had developed. Neoclassical economic theory was built around the laws of supply and demand – 'the market'; in rejecting the assumption of the inviolability of this mechanism, Keynes replaced one reified notion with another. The whole economic structure – 'the economy' – became the new focus of economic wisdom.

The demise of neoclassical economic theory is clearly evident in 'The

Fright that Failed' (figure 10). A jaunty Father Christmas – who, it is worth noting, was, in his present form, the invention of cartoonist Thomas Nast[9] – walks blithely past a half-ghost, half-scarecrow figure labelled 'Slump!' This figure is but a joke; far from being an inevitable and natural force, 'Slump!' can be passed off with a wave of the hand. Goodwill, determination and, more importantly, a relaxation of tight fiscal policy symbolized by the impending carefree Christmas spirit are now the keys to economic recovery.

It is in the mid-1940s that several new elements begin to appear or older, formerly embryonic ones, re-emerge in clear form. First, in 'Unofficial Strike' (figure 11), the cartoon reader is privileged enough to be able to see through to a definite future, to the inevitable consequences of the strike. Yet the protagonists themselves, the workers, are shown once again to have bodily defects, in fact to be manifestly blind to that very future. So by drawing upon a classical theme of European painting since the Middle Ages, that of 'the blind leading the blind', the cartoon has shifted, in this case, the open and even point of view of the vast majority of earlier cartoons. Now, it seems, much depends on where one gazes from – for positions of relative epistemological advantage and disadvantage have opened up. The effect of truth is now no longer got by epistemological consensus but by epistemological differentiation between truth and falsehood.

Secondly, while the worker in 'Unofficial Strike' is clearly shown to be on the side of the natural, he is not represented as *fully* natural. For he is in danger of being overcome by a still more natural force – in this case a flowing river labelled 'economic chaos'. He stands in relation to this abstract concept, then, as the beast does to the wider field. And, while the concept itself is by no means a full-blown instance of the modern use of 'economy' and is, in fact, probably much closer to the traditional usage of the term to mean economizing, it is nevertheless natural rather than synthetic. It represents a danger and can be overcome only by proper use of the human faculties of perception and rationality.

Thirdly, another cartoon from the same year, 1945, 'All Aboard' (figure 12) moves a little closer towards what we have tentatively called an 'aggregation' of the concept of economy. It shows, admittedly, one economic fraction, nationalization, but it is, as the cartoon makes plain, a very big fraction, for it was indeed the economy in its modern sense (or at least key sectors) which was in process of nationalization under Attlee.

Fourthly, the form of this second cartoon is interesting, for it is by now plain that the cartoon realism of the nineteenth century is not the only representational option. Like the pre-realist cartoons (e.g. figure 1), this one is at once sketchy and abstract. Each of its elements is quite carefully drawn where the element in question is central to the theme; yet the elements are collocated in quite counter-realist ways. With regard to forms of representation, then, this is the first truly modern cartoon in our corpus. For distortion and non-realism have become synonymous for the modern reader with cartooning itself, despite the cartoon's long history of realism.

Thus Harrison can write: 'The cartoon is "communication to the quick" because it simplifies and exaggerates; it distills and distorts. The cartoon differs from word or photograph or even realistic line drawings.'[10] 'All Aboard' is perhaps our first cartoon to realize these definitional contingencies: Attlee as captain or ringmaster welcomes aboard the leviathan the Old Lady of Threadneedle Street as well as the industries (mining and railways interestingly represented by their workers). And this sea-monster element is indeed one which crops up in more modern times to represent the economy: the ultimate natural brute which can look tame and civilized under certain circumstances but whose real and fearsome capacities are still quite in evidence.

A complementary cartoon from the same period is 'Rehearsal' from 1947 (figure 13), which, too, shows a quasi-aggregated version of economic life, this time in the form of the Budget represented by a box of snakes, each one of which corresponds to a fiscal, monetary, etc., concept.

Inflation: natural forces and human agency

All epochs appear to have considered *their* inflation as something new and terrible, as the worst ever etc. Three cartoons from the mid-1950s to the early 1960s show three related but distinct ways of combining the (by now) well-known motifs of control and runaway nature around this topic. In the hurricane cartoon from 1955 (figure 14), we see the emergence of the idea that economic formations, while appearing to be quite like natural forces, are in fact the constitutive responsibility of human economic agents. The man and woman in the street compose a spiral of bodies labelled 'wages' (men) and 'prices' (women) – though why this gender division occurs is quite mysterious. This humanly engendered hurricane moves towards and threatens the centre of capital, the City – so we are perhaps to assume that the spiral is primarily the responsibility of the working class.

Yet, in the second cartoon, 'Look out, Mac . . .' (figure 15) from 1957, this notion of agency has been dropped, and we have returned to the representation of economic formations as natural forces rather than human products, even though the creeper is much less catastrophic than the hurricane. The growing spiral of inflation begins to engulf the domestic dwelling (civilization and control). The agent of the state is unable to control this natural spiral, is still grappling with previous lengths when the new growth comes up behind him, and needs to be reminded of this, for his view of things, once more, is partial, while reader, narrator and housewife can plainly see the 'reality'.

By 1960 (figure 16) the organic body is reinvoked, but this time it is not the worker or labour that is associated with the body but British industry as a whole. Inflation is now represented as a disease which can attack the body; it is a highly destructive and recalcitrant part of nature which corrupts civilization and control. Accordingly, the state is now represented as the medical profession, uncertain not just of the cure but, indeed, of the diagnosis. The only perspective in the cartoon that can be given any

REHEARSAL.

"Everything under control?"

Figure 13

HURRICANE REPORTED MOVING TOWARDS THE CITY

Figure 14

"Look out, Mac, here it comes again."

(With acknowledgements to The New Yorker)

Figure 15

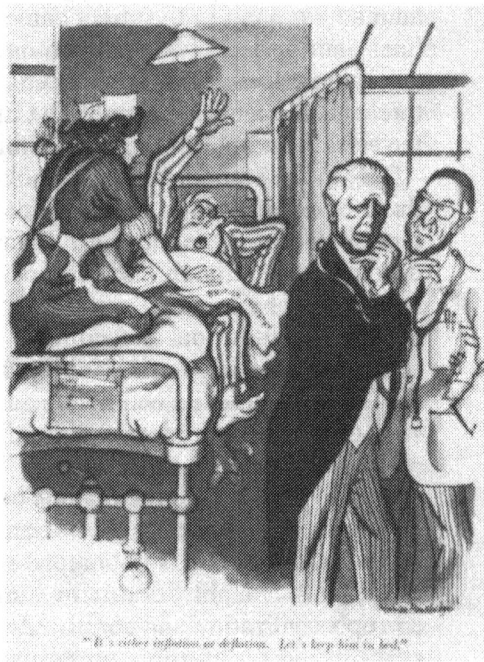

"It's either inflation or deflation. Let's keep him in bed."

Figure 16

credence is that of the patient/body itself, which appears to be quite fit and well and ready to continue if left alone, untouched by the state. The dialectic is between control and its absence, between planned and unplanned economic formations, between free market forces as a positive phenomenon and as a destructive beast: it is this possibility of sliding signification that allows the cartoons to vary their messages greatly with very small shifts of their mythemic elements. In 'Look out, Mac . . .' the state is upbraided for its helplessness in the face of the beast, while in 'It's either inflation . . .' it is upbraided by a *very* similar image for unnecessary economic intervention.

The emergence of the economy

Although the category is discursively available from the 1940s, it is not until the long post-war boom that the economy *qua* economy is finally represented in cartoons. The critical example in our corpus is 'Blossom Time', 1963 (figure 17), the earliest instance to our knowledge of the economy as totality. The Chancellor, Maudling, is depicted as a rotund spring fairy, atop the tree of the economy, bringing, as if by touch of magic, new growth to the orchard. Ostensibly, nature has been brought under rational control by responsible agents. However, what the principal agent cannot see is that the hidden roots of the economy are being gnawed away and undermined by unspecified pests. As we shall see, from this point on, this combination of state and economy is an almost universal feature of the economic cartoon. The configurations and modes of representation may alter somewhat, yet the dominant symbol remains that of the economy as tamed nature but now increasingly susceptible to a number of ills.

By the 1970s, with the onset of a series of economic crises, a variety of representational forms for the economy are pressed into service – snake, horse, fish, etc. – and in each case, although the economy is still shown as a beast, the beast is the passive recipient of either government policy or other less controllable economic contingencies (deficit, inflation, unemployment, and so on). For example, in Pickering's 'Jungle' series from the mid-1970s, the economy is represented by a lugubrious but unpredictable reptile, often proving a problem for government management. However, in the example chosen (figure 18), the economy is on the receiving end of Treasurer Lynch's economic policies. Lynch is shown to take medical over-servicing to a ridiculous extreme, actually creating the condition which he then, somewhat apologetically, seeks to cure. So embedded have medical metaphors for the depiction of economic management become that Pickering is able to dispense with almost all dialogue and explication.

The economy under monetarism

By the late 1970s, both the aggregated economy and, on occasions, its metonymic substitute, the pound, are treated via new arrangements of the mythemic elements we have isolated so far. Prior to the election of the first

BLOSSOM TIME

Figure 17

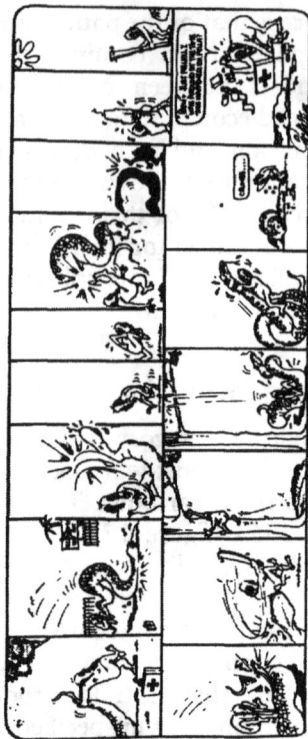

Figure 18

'Hi there, big boy – why don't you pop over and let me make a real man of you'

Figure 19

'Me? Having trouble? How sweet of you to ask – but my horse is only cooling off before the final dash.'

Figure 20

Thatcher government in 1979, one cartoon (figure 19) shows the triplet, pound–body–economy, robust from the Callaghan–Healey years of rebuilding and austerity, now tempted by the free and easy ways of Thatcher's monetarism in the saloon across the way. However, the economy appears to suffer rather than prosper under monetarism. By 1982 (figure 20), for example, it is represented as the skeletal remains of a once industrious workhorse which has become bogged because of a dangerous wrong turn towards Friedmanite policies and the misguided promise of instant prosperity. Thatcher is portrayed as somewhat of an idealist, blithely unaware of the consequences of her actions.

In similar vein, her US counterpart, in another cartoon (figure 21), is shown to be unaware of the real state of affairs concerning the American economy, now portrayed as a dying fish. In the last three examples, then, it is the state which is shown as the ultimate culprit in economic mismanagement. The matter of whether the beast has a life of its own, however, is moot; and so the question of state responsibility remains always contestable on those grounds. The pound–economy figure reappears in 1985 (figure 22), in a cartoon which is almost pre-Keynesian in its representational form; once again it is market forces which are shown to be the determining factor in the economic equation (see figure 8), and monetarism is seen as a form of mystical shamanism taking the tribe to the brink of destruction by malignant natural forces.

Meanwhile, in the USA, the malevolent economic figure has become that of the horned monster of the deficit (figure 23). There is a degree of ambiguity about this monster. She is female and, from time to time, Reagan is shown to be wooing her. However, in this particular instance, his plans are far from romantic in intent but they remain over-idealistic, pinned as they are around the misguided hope that in some unspecified way the diminutive superman, Economy, will outgrow the beast.

Conclusion

While we can make no claims to have discovered immutable laws governing the relations between economy and its forms of representation, we can at least conclude from our investigations that there are specific and conjuncturally related ties between broad economic periods and policies and the particular configurations of relatively stable and standard cartoon mythemes utilized in those periods as forms of representation. We have seen that old elements can re-emerge, that there is no clear and uniform development of relations between economy and representation but rather a more piecemeal inter-articulation, often involving a reasonably long-term delay between changes in the economic structure and their representation.

For example, at the present conjuncture, although Thatcher and Reagan both eschew Keynesian economic assumptions, they are nevertheless still depicted as government (mis)managers of their respective economies, for this has become, by now, an almost obligatory cartoon configuration. To this extent, reading cartoons cannot be a matter of unproblematically

Figure 23

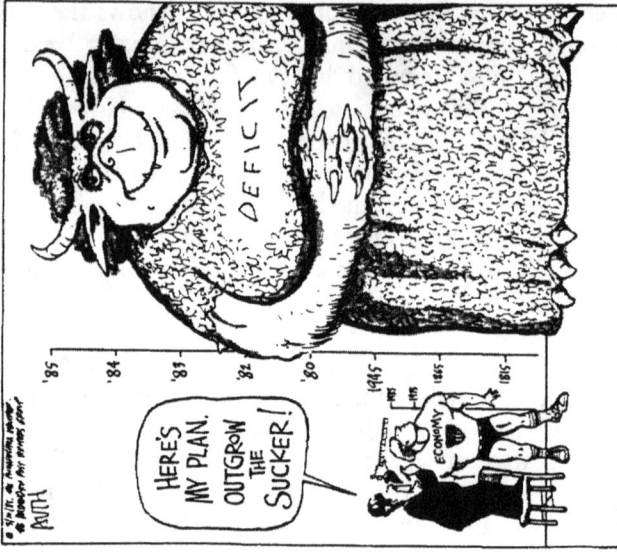

Figure 21

Figure 22

working from cartoon to fixed code and back. If such an operation as 'decoding' is involved, then that operation must entail quite local and particular historical practices and knowledges.

If there remains a trace of what might be called 'universality', then it is to be found in the stability and quasi-grammaticality of the mythemic cartoon elements. However, this possible universality is undercut by the fact that reconfiguration upon reconfiguration of the mythemes is in continual evidence, thereby changing their effective values.[11]

Mike Emmison is at the University of Queensland, St Lucia, Queensland.

Alec McHoul is at James Cook University, Townsville, Queensland.

Notes

1 As, for example, Martin Walker attempts in his collection of twentieth-century British political cartoons, *Daily Sketches: A Cartoon History of British Twentieth Century Politics* (London: Granada, 1978). Indeed, the cartoon has been seen as a political statement *par excellence*. However, while it would be unwise to insist upon too rigid a demarcation of 'the political' from 'the economic', our analytical concerns in this paper are such that the political contexts informing the production of the cartoons we consider can be virtually ignored. For examples of researchers who have considered the cartoon as a form of political representation, see Victor Alba, 'The Mexican Revolution and the cartoon', *Comparative Studies in Society and History*, 9 (1966), pp. 121–36; William A. Coupe, 'The German cartoon and the revolution of 1848', *Comparative Studies in Society and History*, 9 (1966), pp. 137–67; Yeshayahu Nir, 'US involvement in the Middle East conflict in Soviet caricatures', *Journalism Quarterly*, 54 (1977), pp. 697–726; Colin Seymour-Ure, 'How special are cartoonists?', *Twentieth Century Studies* (December 1975), pp. 6–21; and Lawrence Streicher, 'On a theory of political caricature', *Comparative Studies in Society and History*, 9 (1966), pp. 427–45.

2 George du Maurier, *Social Pictorial Satire* (London and New York: Harper, 1898), p. 65.

3 Ibid., p. 76.

4 John Fiske, *Introduction to Communication Studies* (London: Methuen, 1982), p. 54.

5 Du Maurier, op. cit., pp. 127–8.

6 See Mike Emmison, 'The economy: its emergence in media discourse', in Howard Davies and Paul Walton (eds), *Language, Image, Media* (Oxford: Blackwell, 1983), pp. 139–55.

7 For a discussion of some of the early etymological changes concerning the term, see Kurt Singer, 'Oikonomia: an inquiry into the beginnings of economic thought and language', *Kyklos*, 11 (1958), pp. 29–54. The later meaning that 'the economy' has acquired has gone curiously unnoticed. This is the case for even the most astute observers of conceptual and terminological changes. Raymond Williams, for example, fails to include the term 'economy' in his

otherwise excellent collection *Keywords: A Vocabulary of Culture and Society* (London: Fontana, 1983).

8 See John Maynard Keynes, *The General Theory of Employment Interest and Money* (London: Routledge & Kegan Paul, 1936). Keynes, however, should not be regarded as the sole agency in the dissolution of neoclassical economic orthodoxy. The ideas with which he is associated today were to a certain extent already in practice at the time he gave them theoretical expression and were also being advocated by other economists. See, for example, Michal Kalecki, 'Political aspects of full employment', *Political Quarterly*, 14 (1943), pp. 322–31.

9 Randall Harrison, *The Cartoon: Communication to the Quick* (Beverly Hills, Cal., and London: Sage, 1981), p. 75.

10 Ibid., p. 53.

11 Additionally, undertaking this exercise has convinced us that arbitrary separations between economic and cultural domains, evident in some versions of sociology, for example, are impediments to the development of critical positions within social and cultural enquiry.

JOHN FISKE

MIAMI VICE, MIAMI PLEASURE

Top pop songs in the soundtrack and visual style borrowed from rock video and commercials are two of the markers of *Miami Vice*'s distinctiveness from other cop shows. Andrew Ross dismisses the pretentiousness of director Michael Mann's claim to have been influenced by Eisenstein, and instead locates the style firmly in the economic need to win back an audience lost to cable and, after MTV and rock video, too visually literate to find pleasure in the domestic look of network television.[1]

One such pop fragment is described in figure 1. It occurs between two narrative scenes: in the first Crockett and Tubbs are discussing their plans to meet the hoods in a nightclub; in the second they are at the meet in the club.

Shot no.	Shot length (secs)	Description
Part A:	*'Preparation'*	
1	2.0	City skyline at night, tower blocks and lights.
2	3.0	Man's dressing table; arranged on it keys, watch, credit cards, pack of cigarettes and lighter, aftershave, ashtray, wallet. White hand puts cigarette in ashtray and picks up pack of cigarettes and lighter.
3	1.6	Offside rear lights of Ferrari, red and yellow on black.
4	2.4	Black hands rubbing aftershave into their palms

Shot no.	Shot length (secs)	Description
5	2.2	White hands picking up aftershave bottle. Gun visible.
6	1.8	Front wheel of Ferrari at speed.
7	2.0	White hands pick up and flick through roll of banknotes.
8	4.6	Black hands pick up gold necklace and caress it in the fingers.
9	2.8	White hands pick up credit cards.
10	2.5	Shot over Ferrari hood, driving at speed.
11	2.5	Black hands rubbing aftershave into their palms.
12	2.6	White hands picking up aftershave bottle. Gun visible.
13	2.6	Black hands adjust tie knot, big ring visible on finger.
14	2.3	Hub-height shot of front wheel of Ferrari at speed looking forward, passing other traffic.
15	7.8	White hands caress magazine, insert it in gun, check it.
16	5.0	Black hands insert bullets into revolver chamber.
17	2.1	Hub-height shot of Ferrari at speed, looking forward, white-out in lights of approaching car.
18	4.8	White hands pick up and test high-tech radio.
Part B:	'Transference'	
19	7.6	Location shot of Ferrari driving along street.
20	3.0	Shot of Crockett in Ferrari.
21	2.5	Reverse shot of Tubbs in Ferrari.
22	2.5	Shot of Crockett in Ferrari.
23	4.4	Reverse shot of Tubbs in Ferrari.
24	9.8	Location shot of Ferrari driving along street.
25	1.2	Long shot of flashing nightclub lights.
26	1.0	Mid-shot of flashing nightclub lights.
27	1.2	Close-up of flashing nightclub lights.
28	1.0	Extreme close-up of flashing nightclub lights.

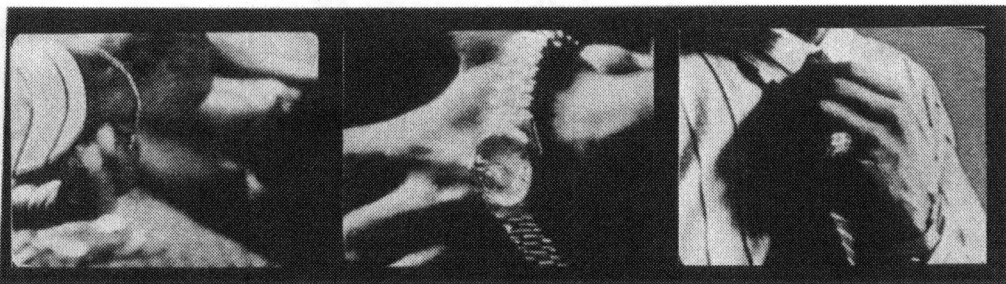

	Length	No. of shots	Average shot length
Whole sequence	1 min 28.8 secs	28	3.2 secs
Part A	54.6 secs	18	3.0 secs
Part B	34.2 secs	10	3.4 secs

Figure 1

Words of lyric

Left home with a friend of mine
Gave two years and I don't know why
Now I'm happy all the time
I can't think and I feel inspired
A girl put me in a situation
I'm going through some permutation
Did you hear me tell the sport
Now you're gonna hear some more
I know a place where dreams get crushed
Hopes are smashed but that ain't much
Voluntary experimentation
I'm going through some permutation

The fragment falls into two parts stylistically. Part A, 'Preparation', is shot in extreme close-up and its eighteen shots are solely of objects that are bearers of high-style, high-tech commodified masculinity. Human hands do appear, identifiable only by skin colour as those of Crockett or Tubbs, but only to handle the objects of style.

In part B, 'Transference', the pop-song soundtrack continues, but the visual style shifts to the more conventional. Their Ferrari is shown on night-time streets in straightforward locating shots (shots 19 and 24) that bracket a sequence of shots and reverse shots (shots 20–3) of Crockett and Tubbs in conventional close-up inside the car. The fragment ends with a

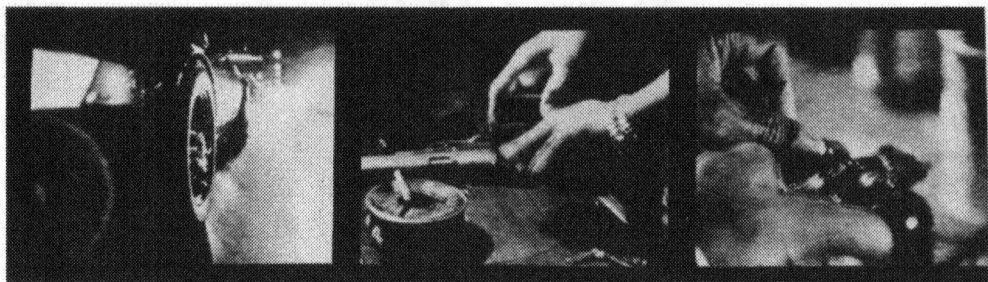

series of quick cuts of nightclub flashing lights in which the camera moves rapidly from long shot to extreme close-up. The shot/reverse shot sequence is longer than conventionally required to establish that Crockett and Tubbs are in the car and to personalize the Ferrari's movement. There is no dialogue to 'time' the cuts; instead the pop song dictates the pace of the editing. Similarly, the move from long shot to extreme close-up in the rapid sequence of shots of the flashing lights not only connotes the speed of their arrival and the urgent, anxious 'feel' of the club, but also visualizes the beat of the music. Part A has the weakest of narrative alibis, not noticeably strengthened by the first line of the lyric; if the scenes on either side of the entire fragment needed a link, part B would have been more than adequate. The fragment interrupts the narrative, as within it the shots of the Ferrari interrupt its own mini-narrative of preparation.

Patricia Mellancamp argues that song-and-dance numbers mirror and disrupt the Hollywood musical.[2] In mirroring they support the dominant ideology; in disrupting they prise it open and leave it vulnerable to crossgrained readings. For Laura Mulvey the visual commodification of the female in classic Hollywood film interrupts the masculine thrust of the narrative, but in her theory there is no hint of the disruptive, only the mirror-image of the fetish supporting the narrative desire.[3] The interruptive fragment of *Miami Vice* mirrors the masculinity of the narrative; it mirrors the commodification of style; it mirrors the high-speed mobility of the Miami world. But does it disrupt?

The pop song, with its driving rap beat, disrupts the diegesis. Unlike theme music, it occurs only once; its references are not to other scenes in the episode, not to other episodes in the series, but to the extra-diegetic world – that is, to the viewer's previous experience of it, and to the domain of pop in general. It disrupts not only the narrative but also television. Its voice is that of a black urban subculture and is thus more likely to articulate the hoods than the agencies of law and order. It loosens Crockett and Tubbs momentarily from their diegetic social authority and allows their style and masculinity to become freely available pleasures, not the free lunch of hegemony.

Television's 'flow' is a constant struggle against fragmentation.[4] TV commercials interrupt the narrative flow; their heroes are objects and their spectators are owners. This fragment is a commercial as much as a rock

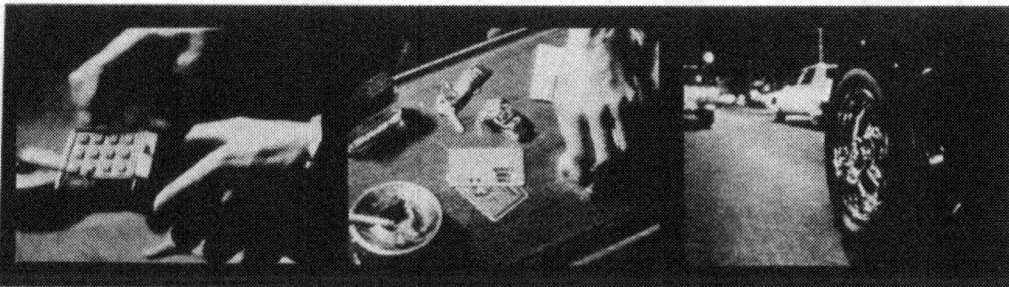

clip. The voluptuous lighting and sensuous close-ups bear the pleasure of ownership. Only the owner sees his objects displayed like this, only the owner's body completes the disembodied hands, only the owner's desire motivates the gaze.

The objects of the desiring gaze are the bearers of masculinity. Margaret Morse and Sandy Flitterman have both argued that 1980s television is capable of turning the male body into the object of gaze, not the subject of action, thus feminizing it, opening it to feminine desire.[5] Here, however, the male body is displaced into its metonymic commodities, so the feminization is not of the body but of the commodity. The feminine is written out, for the masculine is both the subject and the object of the look. That frozen moment when the subject and object of desire merge is the moment of *jouissance*, when power, pleasure and affect liberate the masculine self into its own masculinity, freeing it from the necessity of the feminine. The imaginary of restored masculinity is achievable not through the female, but within masculinity itself.

How central an issue is class here? Bourdieu argues that working-class pleasure lies in an immediate sensuous participation in the object of pleasure: just what this camera offers.[6] Commodities enjoyed as objects, consumed for pleasure, become an excorporated discourse that the subordinate steal from the dominant and use to make their own pleasures, as they steal cars (like Ferraris) for their own *joy* rides.

The car is the ultimate commodity, the ultimate style. It is not just a symbol of male power, of freedom, of mobility; it is the *practice* of power, freedom and speed. The symbol is not a substitute for a lack; it fills that lack. (Car theft is a gender- and class-specific 'crime' – subordinate males practice it.[7]) The Ferrari is more style than function, but the style is its function. Its expense may limit its actual accessibility (in the economic domain), but the style that it speaks can be spoken in more democratic accents.

For the style is all and the style is double-voiced: the reclaimed beach-bum, Crockett, one-time alcoholic with an aversion to socks; and the street-corner 'dude' Tubbs with his mixed-racial origins and his up-to-the-minute dress and music. The style is of the low life become affluent; however Guccified the commodities, the manner of their use bears the accent of deviant, devalued and oppositional voices.

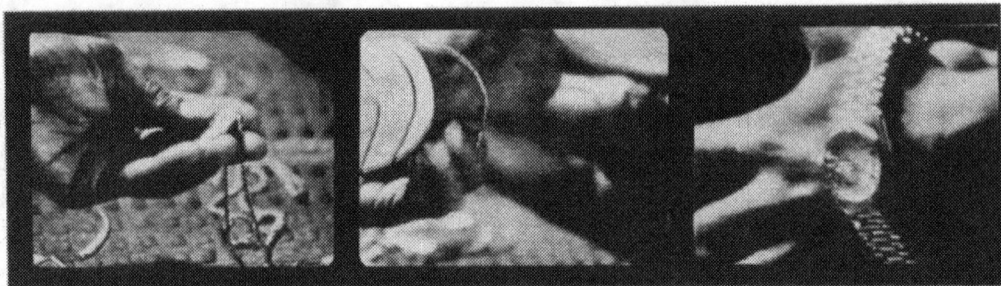

For the powerless, commodities are the access to masculinity: their meanings flow easily from their original economic domain into the more controllable one of style. The circulation of commodities in the market-place is, in the economy of style, the circulation of meanings and identities. For those who reject or are rejected by the system of productive labour, consumption forms their social relations. In the economies of late capitalism, leisure displaces labour, consumption displaces production, and commodities become the instruments of leisure, identity and social relations. (P)leisure lies at the centre of a low-employment, consumerist society.

And consumerism forms the style. Ross reveals how the vice in Miami is 'bad' consumerism. Drugs and pornography are the commodities of pleasure; they are 'the most consummate expression of exchange-value because they do not hide their lack of use-value'.[8] Flaunting the lack of use-value is 'criminal' in capitalism. Commodities of pure pleasure, pure waste, question the norms of the commodity itself, and crack the alibi of capitalism.

In this fragment the commodities of masculinity balance precariously on the boundary between 'good' and 'bad' consumerism. Their pleasure, their waste, is close to that of the bad, as Crockett and Tubbs are close to voicing the underworld they are meant to control. The sensuous materiality of the objects liberate them from their 'good' narrative function. Like the camera of the commercial, the camera pleasures the viewer, the camera consumes them, the camera-consumer. But what is consumed is their sensuality, their lack of meaning, their postmodern rejection of use and of ideology. The camera is a 'bad' consumer. But traces of good consumerism remain; the residue of their use-value lingers on in their signifieds: the pleasure is in the sensualities of the signifiers. The feel of the gold chain as it drapes itself around the wrist, the touch of the fingers against the necklace, the weight of the gun in the hand – these are the pornography, the cocaine, in a post-modern, consumerist world where pleasure is the economy and style its currency. In this world the boundaries are blurred between the good and the bad, the power of the dominant to control slips away as pleasure and style produce a multivocality in which commodities are anybody's speech and not the bearers of a capitalist economy. It's a world of fragments whose democracy lies in their fragmentation.

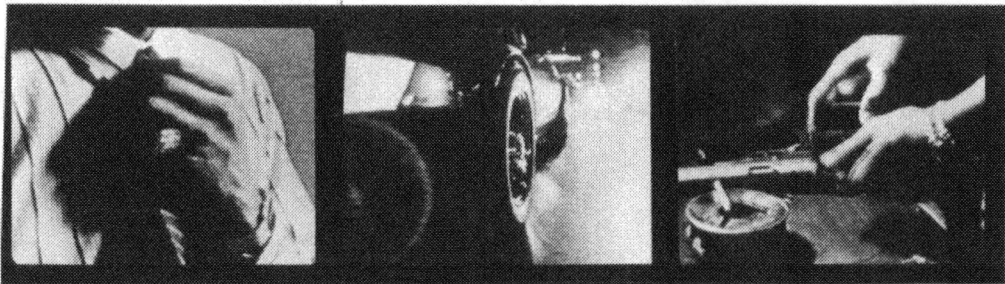

Not that the controlling mechanisms of the cops-and-robbers genre give up so easily. The masculine social narrative constantly reasserts itself, gathers the fragments into its flow, and struggles to regain control. But the disruptive forces are barely contained. The narrative fights to close each episode with a resolution in which sense, control and the masculine are all achieved. However, the style, the music, the look, the interruptions of the narrative remain open, active, disruptive and linger on as the pleasures of *Miami Vice*.

Curtin University of Technology, Perth, Western Australia.

Notes

1 Andrew Ross, 'Miami Vice', *Communication*, 9, 3/4 (1986).
2 Patricia Mellancamp, 'Spectacle and spectator', *Cine-tracts*, 1, 2 (1977), pp. 28–35.
3 Laura Mulvey, 'Visual pleasure and narrative cinema', *Screen*, 16, 3 (1975), pp. 6–18.
4 Raymond Williams, *Television: Technology and Cultural Form* (London: Fontana, 1974).
5 Margaret Morse, 'Sport on television: replay and display', in Ann Kaplan (ed.), *Regarding Television* (Los Angeles, Cal.: American Film Institute/University Publications of America, 1983), pp. 44–66; Sandy Flitterman, 'Thighs and whiskers, the fascination of *Magnum p.i.*', *Screen*, 26, 2 (1985), pp. 42–59.
6 Pierre Bourdieu, 'The aristocracy of culture', *Media, Culture and Society*, 2, 3 (1980), pp. 225–54.
7 Chris Cunneen, 'Working class boys and crime: theorizing the class/gender mix', in Paul Patton and Roger Poole (eds), *War/Masculinity* (Sydney: Intervention Publications, 1985), pp. 80–6.
8 Ross, op. cit.

THE ROAD TO
CULTURAL STUDIES

■ Len Masterman (ed.), *Television Mythologies: Stars, Shows and Signs,* Comedia Series, 24 (London: Comedia/MK Media Press, 1984), 144 pp., £4.95.

I n *Harpers & Queen International* (March 1985) David Cohen introduced its readers to the new translation of Roland Barthes's *The Fashion System.* Fashion, he argued, 'is simply a keyboard of signs from among which an eternal person chooses one day's amusement'.[1] Although this statement is employed to characterize the fashion of clothes, it is equally appropriate to describe the fashion of cultural studies, for the figure is apposite to reflection on the appropriation and deployment of Barthes's notions in the field of cultural and media studies.

In the quest for, and in the guise of, serious academic debate, many of Barthes's endeavours have been stripped and deformed. This is not a novel observation, and considerable debate exists about the cogency of this appropriation and, indeed, about the appropriateness of a Barthesian model. But, given that it has become a widespread practice and presents itself as a coherent methodology, it seems legitimate to look at the arena of its deployment. What one finds is an increasingly frivolous usage in a series of one day's amusements: nowhere is this more apparent than in the recently published collection edited by Len Masterman, *Television Mythologies: Stars, Shows and Signs.* This volume constitutes itself as Britain's companion to Barthes's book on French *Mythologies,* published two decades ago.

There is an irony here. While *Harpers & Queen* presents a lengthy and faithful synopsis of *The Fashion System* for its general readers, without apology or condescension and with reference to examples of fashion in that same issue – deforming the object of consumer choice itself – the Masterman collection constitutes a series of 'excesses', in which the commonsensical and the whimsical are dressed up as the academic with the common touch, ostensibly in the style of Barthes. The difference between the two texts is the presence of an overarching analytical framework in the former, the text for general readership, in the same way that Barthes structured *Mythologies,* moulding his reflections by that framework in the first half and elaborating the model in the second half. In contrast, the

Masterman collection appears as just that: a random set of pieces by different authors on their favourite television programmes. Indeed, the book might better have been titled *Viewers' Choice*. It is prefaced only by a curious introduction which is ostensibly about Barthes but is in fact about British literary studies and their recent disruptions and shifts; fundamentally, it lacks any bridging or locating strategies.

The concept of the book clearly posed intrinsic problems, with its aim of retrospective address, incommensurable cultural milieux, widely various theoretical terrains and twenty-three different authors. One of its most curious features is its lack of attention to Barthes beyond the introduction, or indeed to any other rigorous body of work. The book fails in a number of respects: it is an especially bad example of the genre of 'the collection'; it produces a bad form of pop academia; and it unreflexively indicates the state of the art in the field of cultural and media studies. These tendencies became only too manifest in the series of seminars which were held in March 1985 at the National Film Theatre in London (entry by payment) to signal the publication of the book, and which panned out as merely sites of indulgence for a few armchair reflections and mundane anecdotes – for example, that not even academic analysts can correctly predict future events in soap operas.

There appears to be a peculiar bifurcation on the road to cultural studies, for we find, on the one hand, popular media taking it seriously in certain areas of its work and, on the other, academics offloading complexities and contradictions in the search for popular appeal. This situation seems largely attributable to the centrality of the concept of populism in cultural studies, together with the failure to account for the different registers of the concept. In effect, work in cultural studies has proliferated in quantity and over a broad range of themes, and has increasingly been marked by a desire to be accessible and politically progressive. The sign of accessibility is the lack of a clear principle of selection of objects and themes, other than a broadly leftist critique and a political strategy that promotes a loosely populist politics. Such populism is the most recently articulated variant of a Marxism that turns on a certain notion of class politics in which a working-class consciousness is seen as a coherent entity that potentially challenges the invisible hegemonic grip. In this view, concepts of 'the everyday', 'people', 'popular' and 'nation' have been reclaimed as tools for restructuring society from a classist to a classless one. Thus we find that practitioners of cultural studies have adopted an 'Educating Rita' approach to theoretical work.

The development of cultural studies has seen an uneasy alliance between structuralist and materialist positions, as spelt out by Tony Bennett and Stuart Hall, who adopt a third-way synthesis which overlooks the intrinsic incommensurability of structuralist (or, strictly speaking, idealist) and materialist positions. Rather, incompatibility is 'overcome' by a retreat to the foundations of British cultural studies – the rejection of élite, literary analysis and the assertion of a study of the everyday (the non-élite) marked by a hostility to class, authority and state.

Given the eternal ambiguity of most of the work in cultural studies – namely, an inability to locate the determinants of cultural fields or the forces that shape their tendencies – there is inevitably a retreat to crude Marxism, signalled by the figures of the ruling class, ruling interests, capitalist tendencies, hegemonic domination, and so on. A justification for the existence and operation of these figures remains elusive, or else by implication is treated as obvious. This position is highly unsatisfactory, as is its corollary, the belief that populist politics are the answer.

Nor is all this a trivial problem, as the dispute in the letters page of *The Guardian* concerning the media coverage of the miners' strike has indicated. The positions adopted by those opposing the terms of coverage have amounted to the advocacy of 'sympathetic' representations of the miners, which would be equally one-sided and questionable, since such representations would downplay the actualities of, say, union strategies and forms of action (especially where violence is likely). Such a depiction would be an equally 'distorted' view of strike action, and one, moreover, which would be unacceptable to the majority of viewers. Masterman's own piece on the subject, 'The Battle of Orgreave' (pp. 99–109), illustrates the fallacies of a stark oppositional model, especially in the figure of a police state (of unitary Orwellian proportions) set against a passive, duped public. This line of argument constitutes a primitive and naïve view of how a state and its agents function, evident in Masterman's thin-end-of-the-wedge conclusion: 'public figures can now make unproblematic short-hand reference to picket violence, and be easily and widely understood because a large audience familiar with that view *has already been summoned into existence* by the media' (p. 108; original emphasis). Masterman invokes conspiratorial models of the media which simply do not account for questions about modes of reading or viewing, natures of audiences, disparate registers of violent activities, differential responses to violence, forms of regulation and control in large societies, public opinion, and so on. To put it another way, one could ask what would be an acceptable left-wing line on picketing, limits of picket action, forms of regulation of violence, etc. (see Ian Connell, on pp. 90–2), especially in terms of a 'policy' for media representations.

These remarks are not meant to endorse the usual forms of media coverage and its tendencies, but rather to suggest that the usual terms of opposition are equally problematic, since they turn on promoting a type of coverage which is at least as explicitly one-sided, and therefore easily resisted by existing media institutions and agencies in state bodies. It is of fundamental importance that those engaged in reforming state institutions and agencies come to terms with the complexities of state practices, strategies and policies. Otherwise attempts at intervention can be, and are, thwarted and rejected. The decline of respect for British sociology as a discipline, let alone as a springboard for social policy, after a very brief heyday can be directly related to the naïvety and absurdity of many of the positions that have been adopted in its name and to a general popularizing that has amounted to deskilling and detheorizing.

The result is a form of analysis that is both barren and bankrupt, scarcely able to fulfil its promises. It is a timely lesson that, just as British work in cultural studies has simultaneously proliferated and degenerated, the full English translation of Barthes's seminal work has only now appeared, although his work has been the ostensible source and inspiration for much of the work done in the field. In fact, the field has appropriated elements from a minor, schematic and flippant section of Barthes's work, with scant attention to the fuller ramifications and contextualization of those snippets. The 'Barthes' that has been taken up is but a mere parody of the author.

Such misappropriation is only too evident in the Masterman collection. While it announces itself as a parallel publication to *Mythologies*, it scarcely addresses its quite different context (Britain, not France), its date of publication (1984, not 1957 (English translation 1972)) or its format (many contributors in a series of unrelated pieces, not a multiple exemplification of a closely argued theory). Indeed, the only similarity is the attempt to adopt a frivolous tone – short and snappy. The collection is obsessed not with a comparative study but with its own conditions of production, as if these were somehow comparable. It is obsessed with British literary culture and critique (evident in the Arnold–Leavis recitation) and the assertion of a popular, anti-élitist strategy, but it does not address this specificity with reference to the perceived conditions in which Barthes produced *Mythologies*: those different contexts are not recognized or interrogated, and their effects are not contemplated.

Another fundamental difference is the collection's concern solely with television 'mythologies', a difference which is not adequately addressed in the simple disclaimer that Barthes wrote his book before the rise of television. *Mythologies* may have been written before the growth of television, but Barthes neither revised the book in the light of the television age nor specifically addressed television in later work on cultural forms. This suggests, at a minimum, that he did not consider television to have made other cultural forms insignificant. Yet this is the assumption which underlies Masterman's claim that television easily outdoes all other media in its effortless production of cultural myths, " 'realities' which go – without – saying". The unrivalled mastery of television is explained by describing its processes of production, circulation and effects in terms of class interests, power and élitism versus populism: 'Those with power and authority still manage to have too much untrammelled success for the good of democracy in manufacturing an unspoken form of consent for *their* ways of seeing via television' (p. 6; original emphasis). Televisual representations, then, are reduced to the mere tools of the institutional agents of television, in a form of 'cultural hegemony'.

There are several problems with this argument. Why study television representations at all if it is already known what they 'reflect'? Why and how does demythologization undo this hegemonic domination, and with what consequences? What is the relation between images (representations) and producers and economic/political agents? Fundamentally, Masterman fails to take up the central tenet of Barthes's book, namely the political consequences (effects) of demythologization. Does something change once these ideological strategies are unveiled, revealed and displaced? If not, why not? If so, how? Why can television go on doing the same thing even after it has been 'undone'? What is the status of television among the gamut of other cultural forms? Unfortunately, the contributors to the collection not only do not address these questions but seem not to observe them.

There is one exception. Ian Connell, in a piece entitled, aptly if not ironically, 'Fabulous powers: blaming the media', resists the assumption that 'the media are as potent as is assumed in the claim that they are to blame', a view that is developing even in 'a new generation of socialists' who readily cast the media as one of '*the* mainstays of the present social fabric':

> It recognises no particular political affiliations. If the context is left wing, then it might be the *capitalist* media that are singled out, but those on the right (the Conservative Party, say), and even those who would eschew any kind of overt political affiliations whatsoever (educationists worried about the effects of television on children, perhaps), are just as likely to do the same. The view that the media are biased and to blame for just about any troublesome state of affairs would seem to be a *popular* one. It has become, for many different kinds of groups, a nugget of wisdom, virtually impervious to criticism. (p. 89; original emphasis)

Connell rejects the notions of both omnipotent media and passive audiences, arguing rather that media representations occur within complex viewing conditions – existing sets of questions, queries, beliefs, etc. In the case of the miners' strike, Connell argues:

> The invocation of the media as to blame, as the malevolent manipulator of moderate minds, merely served to obscure, none too well, just how these strained relations between leaders and the (reluctantly) led had developed. It was quite evident that the media did not operate merely to put the miners' case. (They themselves were not above employing a myth or two in their accounts of the strike.) Since they were not explicitly *for* the miners, nor any other group of workers when in dispute, they could be made to seem explicitly *against* them. (p. 91; original emphasis)

Connell rejects the conspiratorial account of the media on the grounds that it explains too little and obscures too much, and that it fails to come to terms with individual and public opinions and tendencies that are already 'in place':

> The suggestion that these feelings and thoughts have simply been imposed on the audience by biased media is, really, little more than a convenient fiction that allows us to avoid confronting the difficulties that arise once we acknowledge our involvement. (p. 93)

In this respect, any myths that television may create and circulate are recognized as such, just as folk stories, parables and thrillers are selectively consumed and processed. Television might be a convenient and ubiquitous form of storytelling (no tribal elder needed here), but there is no evidence from any empirical realm of the effects that are continually asserted to have been produced.

The essential problems of the Masterman collection are its misinterpretation of the notion of mythology and its constant search for some alignment between the televisual and the real. Thus, for example, Charlotte Brunsdon claims that soaps allow 'viewers to become involved in problems, issues and narratives that do touch on our own lives' (p. 87) – irrespective of a dose of *Crossroads*. The quest for alignment displaces attention from the mythic quality of a representation and its place in a system of myths. The Masterman collection would have been vastly improved by cross-cutting its contributions and considering how the programme types considered interrelate and build up into a particular televisual mythic system. This perhaps is the reason why a fashion magazine can successfully incorporate an analysis of the fashion system alongside its regular features and format: because it recognizes precisely its status and format as a mythic production where the alignment between some reality and the mythic is regarded as supremely irrelevant.

Fashion, as a sign system, can never 'deliver the goods', since, as Cohen remarks, 'what is remarkable about this image-system constituted with desire as its goal . . . is that its substance is essentially *intelligible*: it is not the object but the name that creates desire; it is not the dream but the meaning that sells'.[2] Fashion refers 'simultaneously to a dream of identity and a dream of otherness',[3] yet the emphasis is on the fact of dream-ness, for the two can never be realized. That illusion and elusiveness is, for Barthes, the meaning (non-meaning) of fashion, and that is all that need be said. Application of the same criteria by Masterman would have indicated that this kind of book could not be realized.

Griffith University, Brisbane, Queensland.

Notes

1 David Cohen, 'Roland Barthes: *The Fashion System*', *Harpers & Queen International* (March 1985), p. 266.
2 Ibid., p. 159.
3 Ibid., p. 265.

DAVID BIRCH

PUBLISHING POPULISM

- Iain Chambers, *Urban Rhythms: Pop Music and Popular Culture*, Communication and Culture, general editors: Stuart Hall and Paul Walton (London: Macmillan Educational, 1985), 272 pp. £20.00 and £6.95.

- Angela McRobbie and Mica Nava (eds), *Gender and Generation*, Youth Questions, general editors: Philip Cohen and Angela McRobbie (London: Macmillan Educational, 1984), 228 pp. £20.00 and £6.95.

A cademic writing is more and more circumscribed by the method of its production. Publishers want titles that will sell, and academic writers increasingly accommodate their work to the constraints of *laissez-faire* capitalism, often under the guise of arguments about bringing understanding of complex topics to a 'wider and more comprehending community'. This can mean, as is the case with Iain Chambers's book, that the final product is unnecessarily simplistic, theoretically confused, too broad in its sweep through the subject and/or time, and methodologically uncertain in direction and execution. No amount of high-status academic appropriations and referencing (to Barthes or Lyotard) or unspecified quotations (from Nietzsche, Artaud or Breton) is likely to help – particularly in Chambers, where referencing is carried out in a haphazard and idiosyncratic way. People, concepts and terms should not act simply as markers to other disciplines and ways of thinking, but should be a fully necessary and integral part of an interdisciplinarity *required* for understanding a book's argument and position. This is especially true in a book like *Urban Rhythms*, which attempts to develop an interdisciplinary thesis about the relationships between pop music and popular culture.

Iain Chambers, it seems to me, has written two books under the one title: a book about movements in pop music written mainly in the genre of quality contemporary music journalism and supported by an excellent and extremely well-annotated discography (pp. 213–31); and a book about popular culture which for the most part exists in the Introduction, 'Chasing the traces' (pp. xi–xiii), the opening chapter, 'Living in a modern world' (pp. 1–17), the Conclusion, 'In the realm of the possible' (pp. 206–12) and, to a certain extent, in the extensive and often brilliantly illuminating notes and references that accompany each chapter (pp. 232–52). Neither of them works, but separated from each other, re-edited and redirected to appropriate markets, and informed by more coherent theoretical positions (particularly the popular culture one), both would sell. They would fill gaps in important areas, and would allow Chambers to develop his interests rather more fully. Trying, as he does in this book, to relate the two is largely unsuccessful because he has not developed a theoretical and methodological position that would allow him to make the connections, develop the argumentation and give him the vocabulary and theoretical framework to weave the many and various strands that constitute popular music *as* popular culture discourses (rather than to see popular culture as *the* discourse appropriating and *using* the commodity of popular music).

What emerges, then, is a book that implicitly develops a theory of authenticity (as an interesting ironic reversal of Chambers's own refutal of black authenticity in rock) for a particular 'moment' of pop music – progressive white rock. This position seems to be forced upon Chambers by his insistence on viewing history as a series of unfolding events taking place in a linear movement which reaches climaxes or 'moments', and seemingly determined by already headlined media, business and critical interests contemporary to the 'moment'. His chapters are framed by time periods, on the one hand, and by descriptions, on the other, which suggest some sort of teleological progression through those periods: chapter 2, 'A formative movement, 1956–63'; chapter 3, 'Britain's "inner voices", 1963–66'; chapter 4, 'The dream that exploded, 1966–71'; chapter 5, 'Among the fragments, 1971–6'. These chapter headings have their own impelling narrative; a story is being told of birth, life and death – and then resurrection in chapters 6 and 7, 'The release from obscurity: black musics, 1966–76' and 'Urban soundscapes, 1976–'. It's compelling reading at times, with the developing pageant of skiffle, rock 'n' roll, American pop, Mersey Sound, Tin Pan Alley, Northern beat music, blues, R & B, funky music, black music, glam rock, punk, dub, rap and all the other passing moments in Chambers's histories.

This pageant, of course, illustrates the problems of prioritizing certain 'moments', not only because they are prioritized 'simply' as a result of one person's preference over another, or one person's view of history over another, but also because a particular reading of popular culture is made. In this book, it is one that uses subculture theory as the dominant mode of exemplification. Consequently, Chambers's chapters on black music and urban soundscapes (mostly the punk section) are superbly handled – particularly his discussion of the Rastafarian movement – and they are so because these movements are 'made up of' homologies which to some extent are preformed and predetermined by the machinery of subculture theory.

Prioritizing moments of pop music as reactions against a mainstream culture(s) foregrounds notions of alternatives and deviations but leaves the mainstream out of the picture. This is what Chambers does for the most part, thereby creating for himself rather insuperable problems for the development of a thesis about relationships between music and popular culture. It's one thing, it seems to me, to consider progressive white rock as a central current and to highlight developments of different music genres and types, but to do so by cutting the threads of each 'successive' moment, and not keeping in the discussion the continuities, the developments into mainstreams of their own, the relevance of those moments which continue to inform and be a major part of pop music and popular culture (after all, Freddie and the Dreamers and Gerry and the Pacemakers are still doing the rounds) is to fall into the trap of considering popular culture to be reactionary and of the contemporary moment only. The belief, held by many and exemplified in this book, that popular culture came into being only as a reaction against industrialization at the end of the nineteenth century is one of the more nonsensical tenets of some contemporary communication and culture ideologues.

But this is symptomatic of a more ingrained and problematic 'universal' which lies at the heart of structuralist thought and which refuses to die a comfortable but deserved death. If the series editor, Paul Walton, and his preface are anything to go by, this universal still lies at the very centre of the series' and book's aim. He says (p. i) that the series 'aspires to help heal the split between cultures, between the practitioners and the thinkers, between science and art, between the academy and life'.

What split?

More important, perhaps: *whose* split?

'Split', it seems to me, is not just an unhelpful way of looking at different worlds/discourses, but one that positively determines directions of research and thinking into polarized, dichotomized ways of seeing and understanding. It certainly seems to have informed Iain Chambers's way of seeing the world. On one side of a great divide he places pop music and on the other he places popular culture, i.e. ways in which pop music is *used*, thereby creating some mysterious process (never addressed in the book) which results in popular culture. He calls it 'the wider potential of pop' (p. xii). To understand this wider potential, the argument goes, requires a contemporary communication-studies approach to allow music to be 'rescued from a traditional aesthetic vacuum' (p. xii). This will then allow particular sounds (sonorities) to become 'specific indications or symptoms of cultural tendencies weaving across the musical field' (p. xii). But why 'symptoms'? Why just 'indications'? Why does music, and its 'realization' in 'sonorities', need to be kept apart from culture as if it is simply feeding some self-determining, autonomous monster which just happens to change its diet every now and again, but 'in essence' remains the same? It's as if cultural tendencies aren't culture.

Question: when does a tendency become resolved into something more permanent?

Answer: when it becomes culture.

There's an odd sort of syllogism operating here, with old-fashioned structuralist overtones which see 'culture' as some sort of theoretical abstraction *realized* by the 'practice' of such things as pop music. This requires the notion of culture to be some product at the *end* of a process, as part of a developed position, rather than as a dynamic, developing series of positions, so that, as Chambers's book demonstrates so well, some things make it into culture and some don't. Is this really a tenable position? It surely relies on a view of society as somehow monolithic, as being a series of compartmentalized options, as being either/or, like a Hallidayan systems network that offers a series of choices which then gets you access into another set of choices, and so on, until you reach the 'end'. But does the world work like this? The world of Stuart Hall and Paul Walton's Communications and Culture series appears to. They consider linguistics to be esoteric and television exoteric (p. i), and the range of means of communicating can 'at their best blossom into and form an essential part of the (*other*) mysterious concept, *culture*' (p. i). What about means of communicating 'at their worst': don't they make it *into* (sic) culture? Obviously not.

We see this at work in *Urban Rhythms*, which presents a history of pop music based on an élitist network which allows some 'tendencies' to make it and others not. Hence skiffle is described as 'a peculiar British inflection' (p. 39). It took a band like the Beatles to shape R & B into 'an effective cultural form' (p. 65). Buddy Holly, Johnny Tillotson and Bobby Vee (among others) are described as 'insipid sounds' (p. 40). Heavy metal is a 'mutant offspring' of progressive rock (p. 123). R & B groups are 'scruffy' (p. 62), so too the students who go to heavy metal concerts ('The heavy metal audience was (and is) composed of a popular alliance of scruffy students and working class followers' (p. 123)). Popular music and its relations with popular culture in their 'formative years' are seen, *à la* Hoggart, as a predominantly working-class phenomenon ('Rare was the grammar school boy, and even rarer the girl, who could surmount the cultural barriers of their school, family, and social situation and turn to the despised sounds of pop' (p. 29)). Perhaps even more oddly, pop music is considered to be a property of 'youth' ('pop music enters and seals together much of the romantic syntax of youth pleasures' (p. 41)).

Chambers never really tackles a rather more important defining feature of pop music – the simple fact that pop music is an industry controlled in the main by a cartel of five transnational companies who run at least two-thirds of the entire pop market with ever-increasing complications in the 'mechanics of distribution and the high capital investment needed in the new "video market" ' (Jon Savage, *New Statesman*, 17 February 1986). Isn't this popular culture too?

By making subculture theory central to his view of pop music and popular culture, Chambers, like so many subcultural analysts before him, stands aloof from the commercial consequences and defining forms of popular culture. This is not at all unusual, as Erica Carter in her article 'Alice in the Consumer Wonderland: West German case studies in gender and consumer culture', in *Gender and Generation* (pp. 185–214), makes illuminatingly clear:

> Deviance, resistance, autonomy, revolt: in the sociological tradition of the academic Left, these are located beyond the hostile walls of an impassive monolith – the Market. Analyses of subcultural style represented an attempt to freeze commodities-as-signifiers into fixed relations of subversive opposition; the (re)marketing of punk safety-pins and crazy-colour hairstyles was dubbed a 'recuperation' – silencing, defeat. The first punk safety-pin to spill off the end of the mass production line did indeed dislodge punk from its anchorage in the adolescent culture of the urban working classes; yet at the same time it carried the meanings and values of punk into a wider field of teenage mass culture, where its progress has yet to be properly charted. (p. 188)

This position recognizes, and in many ways has been determined by, a need to widen and broaden the scope of cultural studies – not because of apolitical academic reasons, but because most studies of popular culture and youth culture in particular have been male-orientated.

This last comment would be well understood by the contributors to Angela McRobbie and Mica Nava's collection. *Gender and Generation* is part of the series Youth Questions, edited by Philip Cohen and Angela McRobbie, which, like Communication and Culture (both are published by Macmillan), attempts to reach as wide an audience as possible. Rather than directing writers to a particular view of culture, Cohen and McRobbie say of Youth Questions that 'Each book examines a particular aspect of the youth question in depth' and that 'All of them seek to connect their concerns to the major political and intellectual debates that are now taking place about the present crisis and future shape of our society' (p. ii). The particular aspect under scrutiny in the eight papers in this collection is relations *between* boys and girls 'and the ways in which commonplace relations, experiences and representations of youth are quite crucially related to questions of the masculine and the feminine' (p. ix). The major political and intellectual perspective is drawn from feminist directions, chiefly one which emphasizes the marginality of girls and women (Nava, p. 9). The focus is on the notion of gender as a *relational* concept 'of power relations *between* boys and girls' (Nava, p. 13) which results in a feminism that 'does not depend upon the exclusion of boys in order to be feminist' (Nava, p. 23). That position predominates throughout the papers. Mica Nava's opening survey, 'Youth service provision, social order and the question of girls' (pp. 1–30), looks principally at a series of reports on youth and community work in Britain, and adopts a political position within feminism that sees working with only girls as a risk that lies 'in the possible conceptual slippage which can occur between an analysis which perceives girls' needs and interests as different from boys' *now* (because of a range of historical and social factors) and one which asserts a more fundamental and essential difference between boys and girls and men and women' (p. 25). She develops this point rather more fully:

A consequence of an assertion such as the latter by feminists could be to reaffirm a separate feminine sphere within which women become confined – to confirm rather than to attenuate gender as an organising social category. Such a consolidation of gender difference is ultimately self-perpetuating in that it tends to construct masculinity not only as an attribute of all males and undesirable, but also as immutable. In addition, although a feminist approach of this kind may (inconsistently) not assume an essential femininity for girls to parallel its notion of masculinity, it does all the same serve to confirm girls as different, as in some sense victim and in need of protection. (p. 25)

I quote Nava at some length here because it seems important to establish from the very beginning that this collection of papers is an important one and, though varied and rather sketchy in some places, attempts a feminist perspective which is not closed off. Valerie Walkerdine, in an exceptionally well-written paper, 'Some day my prince will come: young girls and the preparation for adolescent sexuality' (pp. 162–84), develops the position: 'Practices which put forward the possibility of alternative literature and images for girls create a set of conflicts and contradictions for girls which often go unrecognised and may in fact make the struggle more difficult' (p. 183). Walkerdine's paper looks at girls' comics and the way they prepare their readers for adolescent sexuality. The argument is a familiar one: girls are presented with and inserted into ideological and discursive positions by practices which position them in meaning and in regimes of truth (p. 162). Where Walkerdine departs from the traditional exemplification of this, however, is to argue that young girls do not necessarily passively adopt a female role model, 'but rather that their adoption of femininity is at best shaky and partial: the result of a struggle in which heterosexuality is achieved as a solution to a set of conflicts and contradictions in familial and other social relations' (p. 163). Girls' comics, she argues, help to resolve the struggle by presenting 'happy ever after' situations, usually involving a 'Mr Right'. Her analysis of stories in *Bunty* and *Tracy* leads her to develop relations between fiction, fantasy and desire, mainly through the work of Lacan (Kristeva is not mentioned), and results in an examination of the constitution of femininity and masculinity 'as not *fixed* or *appropriated*, but *struggled over* in a complex relational dynamic' (pp. 183–4).

Analysis of girls' comics is not new, of course; one of the editors of this collection (Angela McRobbie) has written widely on the subject, mainly in relation to *Jackie*, and, I would want to suggest, with rather more insight than she offers in her paper 'Dance and social fantasy' (pp. 130–61) in this collection. This is an unsatisfying paper in many ways, chiefly because it classifies dance as a social experience into too broad a set of categories: dance as fantasy, dance as image and dance as social activity. It uses the television series *Fame* and the feature film *Flashdance* as data resources in what she calls a 'series of snapshot profiles' (p. 130), which I think presents a much too one-sided and narrow-focused exemplification of dance. True, little has been done in the area, as McRobbie demonstrates in the opening of her paper, so it is an important beginning. But, like many of the papers in this book, this one demonstrates a feature of cultural-practice analysis which is symptomatic of a wider problem. This is a tendency to what might be called analytic parochialism – the unwillingness to extend into methodological areas beyond the 'normal' scope of sociology or visual-image study or appropriated philosophers like Foucault, into such areas as the semiotics of performance, kinesics and paralanguage, which have been developing into extremely useful means of understanding the processes and products of society. Such extensions, say into contemporary (and by that I don't mean old-fashioned structuralist) linguistics, might prevent the rather naïve flirtations with language that often occur, for example:

> Thus we have the experience of dance being linked, linguistically, with the onomatopoeia of the letter F: Saturday Night Fever, Fame, Flashdance – as though, with a quick slip of the tongue, to move rapidly to fever, frenzy, feeling. (p. 134)

If this collection of papers is to be at all useful to students (and that is an aim of the series), then developed methodologies and well-worked-out analytic concepts need to be a part of the work. Everyone needs a vocabulary in order to present insights and observations, and all too often in work like this the vocabulary is not specific enough, thus resulting in a tendency to generalize. Mica Nava's 'Drawing the line: a feminist response to adult–child sexual relations' (pp. 85–111) is a gripping account of a social worker's dilemma in reporting cross-generational sex (between a 14-year-old boy and one of his teachers, a 40-year-old man) and the subsequent traumas that she and the boy went through once they came across bureaucratic red tape, police harassment and the ineluctable grind of education authority procedures. The use of a case study here avoids such generalizations. But, if it is to be used at all successfully as primary data, analytic machinery needs to be set into place. That is not done here, though Nava's reading of the events 'as practices which are above all manifestations of *domination*, and are profoundly intertwined with the social and historical contexts in which children and adults, male and female, are positioned' (p. 109) would suggest that an interdisciplinary model would need to be developed.

Many of the writers in this collection tend towards a generalizing that avoids such interdisciplinary analysis. Barbara Hudson in her paper 'Femininity and adolescence' (pp. 31–53) is a good example. This is an extremely interesting paper, developing, out of Foucault, a discussion of *discourses* which allows her to offer very valuable insights into both femininity and adolescence as discourses. Both discourses, she argues, generate 'sets of stereotypical, generalized ideas which operate as public discourses and which at several points are contradictory and mutually subversive' (p. 49), thus leaving adolescent girls with the dilemma 'Whatever we do, it's always wrong'. Adolescence is a masculine construct, and so images of adolescence are masculine images (p. 35), while femininity is often seen, particularly in schools, as something that 'can be taken on and off by changing clothes' (p. 39). So teenage girls 'find it difficult to know what adults *really* want of them':

> They experience the fact of being judged by two incongruent sets of expectations as the feeling that whatever they do, it is always wrong; a correct impression since so often if they are fulfilling the expectations of femininity they will be disappointing those of adolescence, and vice versa. (p. 53)

But these observations rest on a generality which says rather sweepingly:

> Social workers are generally trying to help girls accept and be confident in their femininity; teachers are more concerned with 'managing' femininity; whereas girls themselves are concerned to be accorded the status 'feminine', a judgement which they cannot bestow on themselves, but must have confirmed by adults and, of course, by boys. (p. 39)

There's another discourse operating here (academic praxis) which Hudson does not address and which, like her arguments about femininity and adolescence, has two faces: the public and the professional. Too often in these papers the public face overrides the professional one – it is easier, and often more persuasive, to present a simplified categorization.

Certainly that is what Julian Wood does in what I think is the worst paper in the book, 'Groping towards sexism: boys' sex talk' (pp. 54–84) (another is Adrian Chappell's 'Family fortunes'). Wood discusses boys' sex talk in a secondary school disruptive unit, and thereby attempts to see in what ways sexism is related to sexuality. It is an account of his observation of 'bundles' among girls and boys in the unit and of his talks with the boys about the bundles (including, among other things, a planned rape of one of the girls which Hudson dismisses as harmless fantasy because it never actually happened in the end!). One example should indicate the standard of this paper:

> The most common simple kind of sexist practice was a sort of feeding off the sight of the girls and of adult women teachers or visitors to the centre. Any slight revelation of flesh (a T-shirt, a skirt) focused the boys' attention on part of the girls' bodies. In fact many hours must have been spent day-dreaming about girls' bodies because at times a boy would come out with an unprompted sexist utterance to the air such as 'tits'! (p. 57)

Are we seriously expected to take this sort of observation as acceptable academic practice?

Adrian Chappell's paper 'Family fortunes: a practical photography project' (pp. 112–29) comments on a project undertaken by one of his students, 'an eighteen-year-old working class girl' in the ILEA's Cockpit Cultural Studies Department. The project consisted of a series of eleven panels of photographs taken and assembled by Tina, and depicting her and her boyfriend's family, together with a commentary by Tina on each of the panels. 'The project enabled Tina to recognize the expectations members of the family held about her own future role as wife, daughter-in-law and mother' (p. 112). For a reason never given, only eight of the eleven panels and commentaries are produced in the paper, and I must admit that I found Adrian Chappell's commentary on how the work came about an unnecessary intrusion. Tina seemed to be doing very well by herself. Panel 7, for example, depicts her boyfriend Mark, with his mother, Pam, cars, a motorbike, Tina and a photograph of Tina and Mark together. Part of Tina's commentary observes:

> This is the way I look at it: I know I mean a lot to Mark, and I know Pam does too. If anything happened to Mark, Pam'd go mad. . . . I think I'd get on better with Mark on my own. Not married to him mind. Mark and me want our own flat. . . . The flat will give me my own ground too, to argue back to Mark. At the moment I can't argue back. (p. 127)

I really don't think we need to be told that Tina's work 'represents an impressive attempt to look into her own domestic life through the use of photographs and words' (p. 126). Primary data can often stand best without comment, and in fact turning her work into an 'academic essay' perpetuates the myth about what constitutes academic writing and editorial expectations. But this is where I came in . . .

Murdoch University, Perth, Western Australia.

For Product Safety Concerns and Information please contact our EU
representative GPSR@taylorandfrancis.com
Taylor & Francis Verlag GmbH, Kaufingerstraße 24, 80331 München, Germany

9 780416 049428